WELCOME TO THE REAL WORLD

'But we can't just let him get away with it –'

'Can't we? You must be new to this, or you'd have realized that there's nothing you can do.'

'Why? How long have you been – how long has he been –'

'Blackmailing me? About eight months.' Her voice sounded calm but moss was flying off the wall in chunks.

'Eight. . . . ? But that's terrible.'

'Oh, you can get used to anything, given time.'

Welcome To The Real World

Ann Coburn

RED FOX

A Red Fox Book
Published by Random House Children's Books
20 Vauxhall Bridge Road, London SW1V 2SA

A division of Random House UK Ltd
London Melbourne Sydney Auckland
Johannesburg and agencies throughout the world

First published in 1992 by The Bodley Head Children's Books

Red Fox edition 1993

Printed and bound in Great Britain by
Cox & Wyman Ltd, Reading, Berkshire

RANDOM HOUSE UK Limited Reg. No. 954009

ISBN 0 09 918831 7

For John, with love

The Kindling

The figure danced in the dark room. It was a clumsy, intense sort of a dance. The head was low, the arms held rigid. All energy was concentrated in the feet as they stamped, stamped, stamped on the bundle that lay crumpled on the floor.

Suddenly, the dance changed. Using one foot to anchor the bundle the figure bent, grabbed handfuls of cloth and arched backwards, pulling hard. A zip gave way with a satisfying rip, but the material itself was too strong to tear. With a cry of rage, the figure tossed the bundle away. It knocked over a metal waste bin and the clang rolled like thunder round the quiet room.

The figure snatched up the waste bin and hugged it to its chest. For ten seconds it crouched there but no other sound disturbed the silence. Satisfied, it retrieved the bundle and forced it into the bin. There was a scrape, then a hiss and a flicker of yellow light.

The match melted a small, round hole in the cloth and produced a sullen twist of smoke, but no flame. A second match widened the hole. The third match fell into the hole and was lost. Frustrated, the figure yanked the bundle out of the bin and held it high. A sudden flame snaked the length of it and bit hard.

With a yelp, it tossed the burning bundle on to a chair. The chair was under a window. Flame leapt up to the curtain and scurried along the weave of the cloth, adding extra little curls of orange to the bright geometry of the pattern. The second curtain flared and growing heat caused a venetian blind behind the curtains to rattle as though a hand was shaking it.

The figure stared, horrified, unable to move until a thick, black greasy coil of smoke reached into its throat, making it double up in a convulsive cough. The burning material had melted away the chair's plastic seat cover and now the foam beneath was well alight. The figure grabbed a sheaf of papers from a nearby table and beat at the chair. All it did was fan the blaze. The papers turned brown and crisp at the edges and began to shoot warning sparks but the figure continued beating in a frenzy of panic until they ignited.

Desperately, the figure clawed a mug from the table and threw cold coffee on to the burning chair. Black fumes ballooned from the foam, sending the figure reeling, racked by a succession of screaming coughs. It gave up then and began to back away, sobbing and shaking its head, holding its hands palm out to the flames, as though to warm them.

Fire began to drip from the ceiling as the polystyrene tiles above the window melted. A light bulb popped and splinters of glass sliced through the thickening smoke. Paint began to blister and curl. The room grew noisy with creaks and bangs and cracklings as the fire took hold . . .

Surname/Family Name: First Name(s): *Rosa Elizabeth*
Morgan

Age: *14* Year: *10* Tutor Group: *10.2*

Home Address:
17 Stanley Road,
Seaton,
ST3 4EN

Telephone Number: *Seaton*
87561

Name of Parent/Guardian Name of Parent/Guardian
Jonathan Morgan *Susan Morgan*

Relationship Relationship
Father *Mother*

Place of Work Place of Work
Seaton College *Seaton College*

Emergency contact name: *Mrs Susan Morgan*
Address: *History Department, Seaton College*

Phone number: *Seaton 50252 ext. 601*

Father's country of origin: *England*

Language spoken at home: *English*

Religion: *None*

Health information: *Registered with Doctor Burton*

Other relevant information:

Surname/Family Name: First Name(s): *Jason*
Hughes

Age: *15*   Year: *11*   Tutor Group: *11.2*
Home Address: *Greenacres,*
Stoneleigh Avenue,
Seaton,
ST6 2LD

Telephone Number: *Seaton*
25667

Name of Parent/Guardian   Name of Parent/Guardian
Joseph Hughes   *Beverly Hughes*

Relationship   Relationship
Father   *Mother*

Place of Work   Place of Work
City Football Club   –

Emergency contact name: *Mrs Beverly Hughes*
Address: *Greenacres, Stoneleigh Avenue, Seaton*

Phone number: *Seaton 25667*

Father's country of origin: *England*

Language spoken at home: *English*

Religion: *Church of England*

Health information: *Registered with Doctor Sutherland*

Other relevant information: *See enclosed reports from private
schools previously attended.*

Seaton Court School and Community College
Student Information Sheet

Surname/Family Name: First Name(s): *Meena Kumari*
Ganatra

Age: *14*   Year: *10*   Tutor Group: *10.3*

Home Address:
112–113, Foleswell Rd
Seaton,
ST2 7XT

Telephone Number: *Seaton*
61185

Name of Parent/Guardian   Name of Parent/Guardian
Ravi Ganatra   *Parvati Ganatra*

Relationship   Relationship
Father   *Mother*

Place of Work   Place of Work
Head Office, Supasave plc   *Head Office, Supasave plc*

Emergency contact name: *Ravi Ganatra*
Address: *112–113, Foleswell Road*

Phone number: *Seaton 61185*

Father's country of origin: *England*

Language spoken at home: *English and Gujerati*

Religion: *Hindu*

Health information: *Registered with Doctor Gupta*

Other relevant information: *See enclosed report from*
Foleswell Junior School.

Surname/Family Name: *O'Donnell*   First Name(s): *Liam*

Age: *14*   Year: *10*   Tutor Group: *10.3*

Home Address:
*72, Tipton Ave.,
Seaton,
ST1 4AB*

Telephone Number: –

Name of Parent/Guardian
Christopher O'Donnell

Name of Parent/Guardian
–

Relationship
Father

Relationship
–

Place of Work

Place of Work

–

–

Emergency contact name:
Christopher O'Donnell

Address: *72, Tipton Ave., Seaton*

Phone number: –

Father's country of origin: *England*

Language spoken at home: *English*

Religion: *Catholic*

Health information: *Registered with Doctor Sewell. Liam suffers from occasional asthma.*

Other relevant information: *Entitled to free meals. Liam's mother died when he was eight. The family has been assigned a social worker. Reports enclosed.*

Surname/Family Name:
Morris

First Name(s): *Christine Jane*

Age: *15* Year: *11*

Tutor Group: *11.4*

Home Address:
*12, Cherry Tree Gardens,
Lakeview Estate,Seaton,
ST11 5AM*

Telephone Number: *Seaton
71565*

Name of Parent/Guardian
Robert Morris

Name of Parent/Guardian
Sandra Morris

Relationship
Father

Relationship
Mother

Place of Work
Saturn Multi-screen Cinema

Place of Work
–

Emergency contact name: *Mrs Sandra Morris*

Address: *12, Cherry Tree Gardens, Lakeview Estate, Seaton*

Phone number: *Seaton 71565*

Father's country of origin: *England*

Language spoken at home: *English*

Religion: *Church of England*

Health information: *Now registered with Doctor Marshall.
See enclosed reports from previous G.P. and Social Services.*

Other relevant information: *Report enclosed from Henry
Parkes Secondary School.*

1
Snapshot

It was evening. Dusk had drained the place of colour, leaving it full of shifting, grey shadows that gathered in corners like fluff. Rosa waited in the angle under the stairs, little more than a small, dark shadow herself. The white streak in her black hair glimmered as she tilted her head, listening. Her eyes glittered as she scanned the hall. On one side, high windows showed trees and bushes, black against a clouded sky. Along the opposite wall, outlines of a row of chairs looked soft and furry in the gloom. A fireplace and three doorways were reduced to blocks of deeper shadow. Straight ahead of her, across an expanse of polished oak floor, a group of display boards were arranged. Each was covered with black and white photographs.

A fierce little wind shook the trees and set the shadows dancing. Then everything was still.

Rosa took a deep breath and glided across the floor to the display boards. The photograph was titled 'Blue'. It showed a boy slouched against a wall, wearing nothing but a pair of jeans. His arms were folded across his chest and he was looking out of the window, his head turned to one side. He looked tense and lonely. Harshly angled lighting added to the mood and defined every muscle. His eye sockets and the hollows of his cheeks and neck were in deep shadow. Even in the darkness of the hall, Rosa could see that it was stunning.

The photograph was stuck to the felt backing with double-sided tape and the ripping noise it made as she eased it away from the board was loud in the silent hall. She bit her lip, gave a final, sharp tug and the photograph tore free.

The noise came as she moved back from the board and she halted in mid-step, recognizing it instantly. It was a tiny sound, but a distinctive one. The squeak of a trainer sole on the polished floor. Rosa turned cold with the knowledge of what she had done.

She whirled, still clutching the photograph, and was caught in a blinding flash of light. Every window bounced the flash back into the hall and, for an instant, it seemed as though the place was full of stars. Then it was dark.

Rosa was too frightened to scream. The cold turned to ice in her stomach. Her mouth was open and her breath came in little gasps. Her blinded eyes were still remembering the flash and saw only two yellow circles, fading to red. The trainers scuffed again, over by the windows. She turned and could make out tree shapes behind glass. Then one of the shapes moved and became a hulking figure, standing a few metres away. As her eyes cleared, Rosa saw that he was smiling and his teeth shone white in the gloom. He tutted slowly, shaking his head, and his smile stretched wider. He held out his hand to show a camera, swinging by its strap.

'Gotcha!' he said.

The ice reached her chest and made breathing difficult. 'Who?. . . . Who?. . . . Who?. . . .'

'Who what? Who let that owl in here?' His tone was creamy with enjoyment, which gave Rosa a spark of anger, and a voice.

'Who the hell are you?'

'Don't you recognize me? I knew you straight away. You're difficult to mistake with that little streak of bird-mess there.' An arm swung up out of the gloom and slapped her across the top of the head, hard enough to make her stagger backwards. She wanted to weep from the shock of it.

'You got a zebra in the family, then?' Blam! The flat of his hand slammed down on her head again, and suddenly she was sitting on the floor. She sobbed once before fury picked her up and set her marching forward. Once again, she couldn't see. Her eyes had recovered from the flash but now they were full of tears. She punched at the air where she thought he was and her knuckles connected with the metal rim of a display board.

'No,' he said, somewhere to her right. 'People with white stripes in their hair shouldn't go in for stealing.'

'I wasn't – ' she began, and stopped as the torch clicked on. The beam wavered across the floor until it found the photograph. It rested there, pointedly. Rosa cradled her throbbing hand and said nothing.

'You should know me, Rosa Morgan. You walk past me most days. You probably don't see me though. I'm like the postman or the milkman. You know, the sort of invisible person the private eye gets dressed up as when he wants to sneak into a place.'

He swung the torch up and held it under his chin, giving a horror-film chuckle. For three awful seconds, Rosa stared at the shadow-mask the torch had created and still couldn't see a face she recognized. Then something glinted in the torch light and she focused on the earring with the silver skull swinging from it.

'D-cup!' she cried, with an equal mixture of relief and anger. D-cup was the school caretaker's son. His real name was Andrew. Andrew Greenwood. And he was right, she probably walked past him without noticing every day of the school year. All she could remember about him now was how he got the nickname. Everyone knew about how he got the nickname. That was a school legend.

It was at a sports day two years before Rosa started at the school. Andrew Greenwood was big even then and Mr Grindley, the P.E. teacher, had lined him up for the shot putt, working on the theory that fat boys had more weight to put behind the throw. As Andrew jiggled his way up to the throwing circle, wearing a very tight T-shirt, the whole school heard Mr Grindley mutter over the P.A. system, 'That boy needs a D-cup.'

Andrew had been in Year Eleven when Rosa came to Seaton and they were still calling him D-cup, but never to his face. He had a reputation as a bully.

Now, his mouth twisted as he flicked the torch beam from under his chin straight into her eyes.

'You shouldn't have called me that,' he snarled from behind the light. 'It's going to cost you more, now.' His voice was so full of poison, it set the skin prickling on her arms and back, but she tried not to show it.

'What on earth are you talking about D-cu. . . . I mean, Andrew?' she asked, with only a slight quaver.

He switched off the torch and took a step forward. Rosa got ready to run but, before she could move, he stopped and picked up the photograph from the floor between them. 'There,' he said, sticking it back on the board. 'It looks as though nothing happened. But I've got a photograph that tells a different story. See?' The torch clicked on again and he held up a polaroid snap of Rosa looking big-eyed and guilty and clutching the photograph like a shield. She winced.

'Give me that,' she pleaded, reaching out a hand.

'Oh, no,' he said, shoving the torch and the snapshot into his camera case. 'I keep it. And unless you bring me a nice, crisp fiver tomorrow, the whole school will come in on Wednesday to find lover boy's portrait gone and my little effort up on the board instead. Get it?'

He sounded so much like a bad American actor that, all of a sudden, Rosa couldn't take him seriously. The whole thing was ridiculous. It was only D-cup, the caretaker's son, and she was acting like a scared rabbit.

'Don't be stupid!' snapped Rosa. 'It's only a photograph. Anyway, I'll tell them I was walking through the hall when I saw it lying on the floor. Yes. And. . . . I was – I was just putting it back when you took a snapshot and threatened to – '

He lunged forward and gripped her upper arms hard enough to stop her in mid-sentence. 'You're not listening properly,' he said softly. 'I'm not threatening – I'm promising. Unless you bring me the money, it will happen. And I know you wouldn't want that. Because it's not just about that photograph, is it?' He shook her, hard. 'Is it? It's about what they'll all think of you when they find out you've got the hots for Jason Hughes after you've spent the last six weeks slagging him off. Yes, I know about that. I get to know everything that happens in this school. Think your image'll stand up to it?'

He chuckled when he saw her face. 'Look at that!' he crowed, grabbing her chin with one hand. 'You've got horror written all over you. Don't ever play poker for money.' He waggled her chin playfully and she winced as the jawbone cracked.

That was when the lights went on. Andrew was good. He didn't let go of Rosa's chin until he had looked up and smiled at the community worker walking into the entrance hall. 'All right, Jim?' he said.

'Hey up!' said Jim. 'Evening classes don't start until seven. What are you two up to in the dark? A bit of slap and tickle?'

'Yeah, something like that,' said Andrew, grinning down at Rosa. She stared back, rubbing her jaw. It was her first, good close-up look at him. He was still overweight, but in a slabby, solid way that made it difficult to tell what was fat and what was muscle. He was at least two metres tall and a mop of frizzy ginger hair added another five centimetres. She looked him up and down for a moment, safe in the bright hall with Jim rattling keys behind her.

'I see you still like the tight T-shirts, D-cup,' she

13

said. Jim gave a short bark of laughter. Andrew's face turned an unpleasant shade of red. His meaty hands flexed, but he could do nothing with a witness standing two metres away.

'I'll see you tomorrow,' he grated.

'Not if I see you first,' Rosa retorted, and she marched out of the door into the thickening dark. She was half way to C Block when Jim's barking laugh rang out again from the open door of the Old House. Rosa stopped dead, imagining the photograph changing hands, the smile spreading across Jim's face.

D-cup must have told him! No, he can't. He wouldn't. But what if he has . . . Rosa groaned softly and shook her head, realizing what power she had given Andrew with that one moment of stupidity. She turned and began the long walk down to the main gates. Suddenly the place she had been a part of for years felt like enemy territory. The muscles between her shoulder blades grew tighter with every step and she kept listening for the soft thud of trainers behind her. The caretaker's bunga-low crouched just inside the main gate and she hurried past with a shudder.

Once outside the school grounds, she let out a great breath and turned to stare back up the hill. The Old House stood at the top, its dark solidity giving the new blocks around it the appearance of Lego constructions. Andrew was nowhere in sight.

The road outside the school gates was tea-time quiet. Rosa could hear the street lights humming and the scrape of a dog's claws as it trotted towards her. In the terraced houses opposite the school,

14

front rooms were lit up and the same newsreader looked out from every television set.

Rosa opened her mouth. 'Blackmail,' she tried. It was such a far-fetched word to be saying in the quiet street that she added, 'Coming to a screen near you soon.' Then a shock-wave of shame and anger poured over her like icy water, making her suck in her breath. She bent over, hugging herself. 'Stupid idiot. You stupid, stupid idiot,' she muttered. 'What are you going to do now? You absolute moron. I can't believe you let yourself get into this!'

The dog crossed to the other side of the road, glancing back, and Rosa realized she was shouting. Hurriedly, she turned for home, letting her feet take care of the familiar walk through darkening streets while her mind went back six weeks to the start of it all.

2
Golden Boy

'It's only grass. And it's damp,' said Rosa, spreading out her coat to sit on.

'I know,' beamed Sophie, 'But it's Year Ten grass. Our grass. No more standing in yard corners for us. I mean look at that. Aren't you glad to be out of it?' Rosa turned to peer at the Lower School yard through the gap between the Old House and C block. The Year Nine boys were making human chains and racing across the tarmac yelling, 'Ci-i-i-i-ty! Ci-i-i-i-ty!'

'Go on,' prodded Sophie. 'Stop trying to look bored. Admit it. You've been looking forward to this, haven't you?'

'Like I said, it's only grass. Why should it be something special just because we can sit here and the younger ones can't? You should ask yourself why they banned the lower school kids in the first place.'

'You know why,' said Sophie, pointing to the gravelled driveway that cut across the grass and ended in a large circle at the foot of the Old House steps. 'They'd only end up having gravel fights or seeing who could make the longest skid marks. We're more responsible.'

'No,' Rosa shook her head. 'Divide and rule, that's what it is. We stay happy because the teachers have given us our little privileges and in return we do their policing for them.'

'Policing? Us?'

'Yes. Us. Can you imagine the uproar if any lower school kid tried to set foot on this grass now?'

'Oh, Lord. Spot the lecturer's daughter,' drawled Natalie Cooke, shaking back her long, fair hair and lifting her face to the sun.

'Well, I've been looking forward to this,' said Sophie, undaunted, and she sat down with a satisfied grin. Watching her, Rosa felt a twinge of envy. Sophie didn't seem to notice that, while the Year Ten girls were all gathered on the grass like a flock of self-conscious starlings, the Year Elevens had made a point of staying away. Rosa could see them at the windows of C block, pointing and sneering. She was gripped by a sudden, fierce desire to be somewhere else. Someone else.

'And I'm looking forward to sharing C block with Year Eleven,' continued Sophie. 'We'll be in the poshest part of the school, right next to the theatre and the community lounge and the cafeteria – '

'Trust Sophie the sofa to be thinking about food,' said Natalie. Sophie's smile fell off her face. She pulled her skirt down over her knees and folded her arms across her stomach.

'But I wasn't thinking about food – '

'Only joking, Soph,' said Natalie. 'Can't you take a joke? Anyway, why all the fuss about C block? The Old House is the best place in this dump. The A-level lot are so lucky to be there. Imagine, your own common room, with posters on the walls and

17

armchairs and a carpet. They've even got a little kitchen.'

'Oh, shut up, Natalie,' snapped Rosa, glad of a reason to be angry. 'You've only been in Year Ten for five minutes and you're wanting to move on. You've always been the same. As soon as you get one thing, you're after the next. It must be hell in your house on Boxing Day.'

'Don't you tell me to shut up, Rosa Morgan!'

'Don't say stupid things, then,' said Rosa. She turned her back on Natalie's furious face and glared at the Old House. She had to admit that Natalie had a point about it being the best place in the school. It had a huge, square entrance hall, with oak pannelled walls and a fireplace big enough to stand in. A staircase with carved, oak bannisters dog-legged in four flights all the way up from the entrance hall to the attic rooms where they had English lessons. Each flight was guarded by two little carved lions, one at the bottom and one at the top. They sat on the bannisters and glared. Their heads were dark and shiny from years of people reaching out to stroke the smooth wood as they climbed the stairs.

One of the best Old House ghost stories was about those stair lions. One night, when the house was still a family home, a young kitchen maid crept out of her attic bedroom. She was crying. She stood for a moment in her white nightgown, staring into the moonlit hall below, then she climbed on to the bannister rail and threw herself down the stairwell. When she jumped, she gave a terrible scream and all the lions turned their wooden heads to watch her fall.

Rosa had been told that story in her first year at Seaton and for weeks her dreams had been full of the splintering creak of wood as the lions lifted their faces to the roof and blinked their blind, carved eyes into life.

Now, she shuddered in the mild sunshine, remembering the nightmares. I must be the only person in the history of the school never to have touched the stair lions, she thought, staring at the Old House.

At that moment Mrs Grayling, the Head of Year Eleven, came out of the front door and, walking beside her, was a boy. Rosa forgot how to breathe. He was perfect. From his thick, blond, sun-streaked hair to his soft, brown leather boots, he was perfect and Rosa was filled with a longing so strong there was no room for anything else. It seemed to her that the whole school came to a stop as he walked over to C block.

'Ohhhh,' breathed Natalie Cooke and Rosa's brain came back to life. Quickly, she shut her mouth and glanced at the others, but they hadn't noticed. They were all staring at him too.

Just then, he looked across and waved. Rosa set about picking bits of grass from her skirt, but the others kept right on staring. He grinned and moved on, walking like his own personal red carpet was unrolling in front of him all the way. Just before he disappeared into C block, Natalie stuck her fingers in her mouth and let rip with a long, lustful wolf whistle. He blew a kiss at her over his shoulder without even breaking his stride.

That was when Rosa began to get angry. She was angry with the boy for being so arrogant. She was angry with the others for letting him see the effect he was having. Most of all, she was angry with herself for not living up to her reputation. Rosa was proud of her reputation. She had been building it up stone by stone since her first day at Seaton, until now it encircled her like a turret and she was safe inside. Everyone at Seaton looked at the turret and thought they were seeing her; Rosa the intellectual, in control of her life, too busy being clever to have time for boys. Now, it was as though this boy had reached over the top of the turret and pulled her out. Rosa felt exposed.

'Who was he?' moaned Sophie Sullivan, still gazing at the swinging doors of C block.

'That was Jason Hughes,' said Natalie, always the first in the class to know anything. 'You know, Hughesie's son.'

Everyone looked terribly impressed. 'Hughesie?' asked Rosa, trying to sound bored.

'Oh, Rosa, you're hopeless,' groaned Sophie. 'She's talking about Joey Hughes. The footballer? He's captain of the City.'

'Oh.'

'They live in one of those big houses along Stone-leigh Avenue,' continued Natalie. 'My mum's friend cleans for them.'

'I wonder what he's doing here?' said Sophie.

'I know,' said Natalie, with a smug little smile.

'Natalie, you pig! I was round your house last night and you didn't say a word!'

'Well, I didn't know he was going to look like that, did I? Anyway, now I've seen him, I might just keep it to myself. Knowledge is power and all that. . . .'

'Oh, yeah? And unity is strength,' said Sophie, scrambling to her feet. 'Come on, you lot. Remember what we did to her on her last birthday?'

'OK, OK,' said Natalie, hastily. 'I'll tell you. My mum's friend says they've run out of boarding schools to send him to. He's been chucked out of them all. Well, three. I heard he broke into the new school swimming pool at one place, just before the opening ceremony. He filled it up with red dye and floated a shop dummy face down in the middle!'

'What!'

'It's true! He got expelled from the last school for writing what he thought of the games teacher.'

'Sounds a bit hard, expelling him just for that,' said Sophie.

'Well, he did write it all over the cricket pitch with nitric acid. So, anyway,' Natalie paused for maximum effect, 'he's going to be coming here. In Year Eleven. In the same block as us!'

Rosa listened to the talk of blue eyes and blond hair and expensive clothes until she could stand it no more.

'Will you lot just shut up?' she said. It came out a lot scratchier than she meant it to. 'I mean, appearances and clothes – they're not important. Just packaging!' Rosa tried to smile, but her face was already too busy scowling. She was still floundering after that first sight of Jason and, when she floundered, she fought. She couldn't help it.

'Why is it that the ones who say looks don't matter are always, for instance, slim and tiny with lots of dramatically black curly hair?' asked Sophie, who was plump and ginger and looked as though she had been taken out of the oven too early. She grinned at Rosa and Rosa grinned back and the atmosphere lifted.

'You could make a dustbin bag look stylish. In fact,' continued Sophie, 'you even looked great in those horrible nightdresses we made in the top year of juniors. Do you remember?'

'Oh, God, yes! We were forced to do a fashion show round all the classrooms, and Sheila Dodd got so nervous, she was sick all down the front of hers.' They leaned together, laughing, and Sophie touched Rosa's arm. The touch took Rosa back to summer days at junior school, when they had been best friends and life had been simple. Things had changed when they came to Seaton. Rosa had turned prickly and awkward, suddenly more concerned with doing well than having fun, and Sophie had slowly drifted away into Natalie's group.

'Don't you try to tell me clothes aren't important, Rosa Morgan,' pouted Natalie, still smarting from being told to shut up. 'Look at you! Always in black – except for that stupid white streak in your hair – with your jangly earrings and your campaign badges and your National Health reading glasses. . . . Don't tell me you haven't thought about your image. You wouldn't wear just anything, would you?'

'Hey! That's not fair, what you said about my white streak. You make it sound as though I bleach it in or something.'

'Yeah, come on, Natalie,' said Sophie. 'You know she's had that streak since she hit her head on the fireplace kerb when she was little – '

' – and she had to have stitches and when the hair grew back in, it was white. I know, I know,'

22

Natalie cut in, rolling her eyes and giving an exaggerated yawn.

'Do you remember all that trouble you had when we started at Seaton, Rosa?' said Sophie, with a slightly desperate laugh. 'We all had this craze for putting different coloured streaks in our hair and you spent your first week telling the teachers that you couldn't go home and wash it out because it was natural.'

Rosa smiled at Sophie to show she remembered but she refused to be distracted from the argument. She turned back to Natalie. 'Look, I'm not saying people shouldn't care what they wear. You're right, I wouldn't wear just anything. What I'm saying is, it's all just a shell, isn't it? I mean, this Jason Hughes could be a really nasty character for all you know. It's what's underneath the shell that counts.'

'I wouldn't mind looking underneath his shell,' breathed Sophie. 'What about you, Natalie?'

'Oh, yes. All that smooth, brown skin – '

'Of course he's brown!' shouted Rosa. 'He's rich, isn't he? He's probably been in the Seychelles all summer. That's what money can – '

'Oh no. No thank you,' interrupted Natalie. 'I'm not starting off the term with a lecture from Red Rosa. I'm off. Who's coming to see where he went?'

They all got up and followed her, even Sophie, after an apologetic little shrug.

'Don't call me Red Rosa!' yelled Rosa, furiously. She hated that nick-name. She had been stuck with it ever since Year Seven when Mrs Sanderson had put 'Community' on the board and told the class to write down what it meant. Rosa could still remember what she had written.

"To be a community means you should not let old ladies freeze to death while you use lots of electric for Christmas lights in your precincts. To be a community you should not put nuclear stuff in the sea so that little children building sand castles get cancer. Community means you look after people."

Mrs Sanderson had read it out in class and Rosa's fate was sealed. That was the worst thing about Seaton Court. If you didn't trundle along being just like everyone else, you got labelled as some sort of a lunatic.

Natalie was nearly at the doors of C block before Rosa calmed down enough to think of a good parting shot. She stood up and yelled, 'Hey, Natalie! Don't get too attached to golden boy, will you? Because if his parents can't even pay people to put up with him, then he won't last two minutes here!'

Rosa was wrong. The whole school went crazy over Jason Hughes. The Year Ten girls spent their breaks arranging themselves in fetching positions on the grass outside his formroom and the Year Eleven girls did exactly the same thing inside his formroom. It wasn't just the girls. There were always little crowds of football groupies hanging around, listening to stories about Jason and his dad and the City, and all the wild times they had together. Natalie Cooke was acting like a little puppy. She would hang around, flinging back her long, fair hair and waggling her backside until he tossed a few words to her. Then she would scamper off to her friends to tell them what he'd said. Rosa came across them a few times down by the Year

Ten lockers, listening to the latest episode of the Jason and Natalie saga.

Jason Hughes lapped it up. He didn't care who was surrounding him, as long as he was the smiling centre. Rosa watched as he walked around the school, handing out charm like a chocolate machine. They all scurried away with their ten-pence worth and no one seemed to notice that none of it touched him: they were forgotten as soon as they moved out of orbit.

Rosa stood on the sidelines, refusing to play the game and mocking them all for being such push-overs. People soon expected it, just like they expected her to argue with Mrs Sanderson in Social Studies lessons or refuse to cook anything with meat in it in Home Economics. It was her job.

Once, Rosa even managed to fool herself. It lasted for three days, until he walked into the cafeteria and sat at the next table, back to back with her. She couldn't finish her vegeburger. He was boasting about the race horse his dad had a part share in and, as he talked, he kept tipping his chair back until it touched hers. He smelled wonderful. Clean cotton and pine needles.

When he reached over and took her salt without even asking, Rosa turned and gave him the blackest scowl she could manage but, for the rest of that afternoon, she kept remembering how his hand had closed round the little pot of salt. She kept seeing the brown skin and the tendons flexing and his fingernails all smooth and clean and beautifully squared off at the ends.

Things began to calm down after a couple of weeks. The term got underway and time was filled up with school activities and homework. For a while the school was nearly back to normal. Then, five weeks into the term, a display went up in the entrance hall of the Old House. It had been put together by the school photography group and it was called 'Portraits'.

'Oh, go on, Rosa,' said Sophie, stopping at the bottom of the Old House stairs. 'Don't be so stubborn. Just one look. They're great photographs.'

Rosa glared over at the boards displaying the 'Portraits' photographs. A crowd had gathered in front of Pamela Weston's studies of Jason Hughes. 'You know, I feel sorry for that photography group,' she said. 'They probably all worked really hard on their portraits, but they could have saved themselves the bother, because dear old Jason has stolen the show.'

'Come on,' grinned Sophie. 'Take a look. You know you want to, really.'

'I'd rather eat worms.'

Now Rosa groaned, remembering how she had sent the words echoing across the entrance hall, turning heads. She couldn't let Andrew broadcast the truth. What would they all think of her?

'You're late,' said her dad when Rosa pushed open the back door. She stood still, struggling with a desire to fling herself on to his knee and howl out the whole story.

'I told you I was staying behind to help Mrs Sanderson do her wall display,' she said, surprised to hear a normal voice come out of her mouth.

'Oh, yes. You look awful,' he added, peering round the side of his *Guardian*.

'I. . . . I only meant to look. . . .' she faltered and tailed off. Her throat closed up. She clutched her school bag, frozen.

'Pardon?' frowned her dad, letting the paper fall. He was half out of his chair when her mother dashed in, stuffing papers into her briefcase ready for an evening lecture.

'What's the matter, Rosa,' she demanded. 'Don't you feel well?' Her cool hand rested on Rosa's forehead for an instant and she tried to look concerned but her voice had tightened with a twist of irritation. Rosa straightened her shoulders.

'Don't worry, Mum. I'm not going to be ill on you. I'm just a bit tired. I was up late last night, working on a tough essay.'

'And did you crack it?'

'Just about. I'll go and put in a bit of time on the word-processor before supper.'

'That's my girl,' said her mum, proudly. Rosa backed out of the kitchen and headed for her room.

>Insert a disc
>Opening document file
>File name: Rosa

I nearly blew it then. If mum hadn't come in and done her busy career woman bit, I would have told them. And I can't do that.

Why not?

Because I'd die of shame, stupid.

Oh, God. Why did I do it? I can't believe I did it. I only meant to look. I've never stolen anything in my life before, not even the penny bubblies everyone used to nick from the corner shop just for the dare of it. Stupid, stupid, stupid!

I hate him for doing this. I HATE HIM. I won't just give in to a slob like him. He can show the whole school his poxy photo – I don't care what they think of me.

Yes I do. I couldn't face them if they found out. And if Jason Hughes heard about it, I'd die.

I've got to get that photograph off D-cup.

Right. What to do. Take five pounds out of my CD Player fund. Give him the money, get the photograph. Those Polaroid cameras don't do negatives, so that'll be the end of it. It'll teach me never to be so stupid again.

I'd like to kill him.

>Delete File Name: Rosa
>Are you sure? Yes/No
>Yes

3
Control

'Get it over here, now!'

Rosa felt her heart clench. She turned, her hand reaching for the five pound note in her coat pocket.

'To me! To me!' The footballers surged away across the lower school yard and Rosa glared after them, while she waited for the blood to stop pounding in her ears. Where was he? She had skipped breakfast and come into school early, wanting it over with before the crowds arrived, but after half an hour of pacing corridors and dodging teachers, she still had not found him and the bell was about to go.

Rosa turned her back on the yard and stared through the gap between the new sports complex and the back of C block. She could just see the red tiled roof of the caretaker's bungalow down by the main gate. He must be in there, she thought. In bed. Snoring. And I didn't sleep all night. She closed her tired eyes and tried to ignore the sick emptiness in her stomach. The sun had not reached the corner of the yard where she stood and she shivered in the cold, crisp air.

'Someone just walked over your grave, bird-mess,' hissed Andrew, a centimetre from her ear.

Rosa jumped and a rabbity little squeak popped out of her mouth before she could stop it. When she turned round, he was smiling. She glared into his pale blue eyes, letting the anger blaze out, but his smile only stretched wider.

'It's been fun, watching you scurry about looking for me. Don't do it again, though. This is my patch. I do the hunting round here. Now, Uncle Andrew wants his present, bird-mess. Bring it round to the back of the Old House at break.'

Before Rosa could answer, the bell went for the start of school and he sauntered off across the yard, right through the football game. They didn't protest, not even when he kicked apart the pile of coats that marked one goal post. The footballers gathered up their things in silence, refusing to look at one another and Rosa suddenly understood how alone she was. All the anger drained out of her, leaving a cold and empty space.

The little yard at the back of the Old House was out of bounds because that was where the big metal school bins were kept. When Rosa crept round the corner at break, it was deserted. The main school hall had been built hard up against the Old House and its windowless back wall loomed over the yard, blocking out the sun. The smell from the bins lolled on the sluggish air and green slime coated the damp concrete. Rosa walked into the middle of the yard, listening to the hollow little tock each footstep made. She stopped and waited, with her arms hanging at her sides, and the cold, empty space inside her grew bigger.

When a door opened behind her, she froze, waiting for an angry voice to shout, 'Out of bounds!'

'Come on then, bird-mess. I can't wait all day,' said Andrew. He was leaning up against a green painted doorframe. The door was open behind him and light shone out soft and golden, making the yard seem even more cold and dark. As Rosa walked towards him, she could see a metal handrail and concrete steps going down. The air coming up from the basement was dry and warm.

Andrew held out his hand. Rosa fished out her five pound note and looked at it. She had trudged along rainy streets with a newspaper sack cutting into her shoulder to earn that five pounds. She had climbed out of a warm bed to fight with garden gates and get her fingers chewed in spring-loaded letter boxes. And now all he had to do was hold out his hand. A little spark of anger began to zip around inside her but she squashed it down. She just wanted the whole thing over. She swallowed hard and put the money into his palm.

'Oh, for me?' he simpered, in a high voice, fluttering his stunted, sandy lashes. 'Why, thank you. Now, get lost,' he snarled and stepped back, slamming the door in her face.

For a few seconds Rosa stood, staring at the cracked green paint. Then the anger flared up. 'Come out of there!' she roared, pounding the wood with her fists.

Instantly, the door opened. He was right behind it with a smirk on his face. 'Yes?' he said.

'Don't you play games with me!' shouted Rosa. 'Where's that photograph?'

'Somewhere safe,' he said, still smirking.

31

With a great effort, Rosa lowered her voice and tried again. 'Look. I gave you the money. Now you give me the photograph. That was the deal.'

The smirk became a grin. 'Oh, no, no, no, no,' he explained, patiently. 'The deal is this. I get the money. I keep the photograph.'

'But – that's not fair.'

'Welcome to the real world,' said Andrew, starting to shut the door again.

'You lying slug!' yelled Rosa, jamming the door with her foot. Her fists flew up to thump him but, lizard-quick, his big hands clamped on her wrists. He squeezed until her fists fell open. A pause, while he checked the Old House windows for watchers, then, with a deft precision, he changed his grip from her wrists to her little fingers. One swift twist and her fingers were bent back as far as they would go.

Suddenly Rosa forgot all about the photograph and her image. The only thing she cared about was stopping the pain. When he slowly guided her fingers down towards the ground, her whole body followed in a careful curve, until she was kneeling on the wet concrete.

He brought his face down close and she saw through tears of pain that he had switched moods like television channels. The smirk had gone, replaced by a snarl of rage. Fear iced her spine.

'Listen to me, bird-mess,' he grated. 'I never said you would get the photograph. The fiver was to stop me putting it on the board, remember? Now stop calling me a liar and start giving me some respect!' He shouted the last word, at the same time giving her fingers a final, vicious wrench. Then he let go. 'I'll be in touch, bird-mess.'

Rosa heard the door slam but she didn't look up. She was too busy cradling one hand in each armpit, waiting for the pain to stop.

'Are you all right, Rosa?'

Rosa lifted her head from the desk, blinking back tears. Mrs Sanderson was hovering in the doorway. ' – Fine! I'm fine. I was just . . . resting my eyes for a minute. I thought everyone had gone.'

'I see. Are you sure nothing's wrong, dear? It's not like you to miss out on a class discussion.'

Rosa pushed herself up from the chair. The throbbing ache in her fingers flared into pain and she winced. Mrs Sanderson frowned, staring at the streaks of green slime on her school skirt. 'Rosa – '

'I – fell over, Miss.'

'You – fell over. Aha.'

'Yes. At break. So I was, well, a bit shaky in the lesson. That's why I didn't join in. . . .'

Mrs Sanderson pursed her lips and watched Rosa for a few seconds longer, then she said, 'Fair enough. Stay here if you want a quiet sit down. If anyone asks, you're doing a job for me.'

'Thank you, Miss.'

Rosa stayed upright and smiling until the door closed, then she slumped. Idiot! she thought. First you get Dad wanting to know what's wrong and now Mrs Sanderson. D-cup won't need to stick his stupid photo on the board if you keep this up.

She sighed and hooked a finger under her shirt collar, pulling out an engraved silver locket on a chain. It was smooth and warm in her palm and she clasped it for a moment, finding comfort in the pleasing shape. When she opened the locket, her mother and grandmother stared out with the same deep blue eyes, from under the same heavy, black fringe. The two photographs had been taken a generation apart, yet both women faced the camera with the same expression. Control, the expressions said. We are in control of our lives.

Rosa's mother had given her the locket the night before she started at Seaton Court. 'Remember, Rosa,' she said, 'Your great grandmother was a self-educated woman, your gran went to university and so did I. I'm hoping you'll carry on the tradition. Seaton Court's a good school but it's up to you to take what you want from it. You're the one in the driving seat. Only you can control your life. I'm sure we'll be proud of –'

Rosa snapped shut the locket. She wasn't controlling her life. Not any more. Andrew Greenwood was in the driving seat and she had put him there.

She sucked in her breath, jumped up and ran to the window. The long sweep of playing fields stretched out below her, leading down to the main gate and the caretaker's bungalow. Rosa stared, trying to wipe from her brain the image of Andrew's snapshot lined up alongside the photographs of Mum and Gran. She leaned forward to rest her head against the cool glass and he came walking out of the bungalow and looked up in the direction of C-block. Rosa knew she would be a mere smudge at a window from that distance, but still she froze until he hitched his jeans up over his belly, looked at his watch, and strolled over to the main gate. Rosa straightened up and took a deep breath. Her hands were shaking.

Andrew planted himself in the middle of the

pavement, facing the gates, with his legs apart and his arms folded across his chest. One after another, the long straggle of people coming back to school after lunch veered off the pavement and into the road, rather than push past him. The groups of bigger boys lasted out the longest, but the end result was always the same. They kept their heads down afterwards, which made them look smaller, as though he had stolen a part of them.

Rosa clenched her fists, ignoring the yelp of pain from her wrenched fingers. Surely someone would stand up to him? Then she saw Meena Ganatra walk through the gates and on up the path with a straight back and a clear, steady gaze. Meena stopped squarely in front of Andrew and Rosa tensed, willing him to step aside. Instead he turned, draped an arm around Meena's shoulders and guided her behind his garden fence. It was difficult to tell from such a distance, but he seemed to be talking and smiling.

Rosa was stunned. Clever, pretty Meena was his girlfriend? She kept staring as they stood close together behind the fence, out of sight of the school road. Meena reached into her briefcase, brought out a white carrier bag and pushed it at his chest. It was when he trapped Meena's jaw in one large hand, tilting her face upwards, that Rosa suddenly realized what was really happening. Even before Meena pulled away and hurried back to the path, rubbing her chin, Rosa knew. Horrified, she touched the bruised place on her own jaw and thought, I'm not the only one. . . .

The classroom door snicked open behind her.

Rosa grabbed a pile of text books from the sill and hurried towards the stock-cupboard, head down.

'It's only me.'

'Oh, hi Sophie!' trilled Rosa. 'I'm just doing a job for Mrs Sanderson. . . .'

'Right.' Sophie stood on one foot, hooking the other leg round her calf. 'I thought I might find you up here. Um. I just wanted to make sure – to check -' Wordless, she nodded at the green-stained skirt.

'Check what, Soph?' smiled Rosa, her voice as sweet and brittle as spun sugar.

Sophie balanced desperately. 'Swapsies?' she blurted, waving a lunch-box.

Swapsies. For an instant, Rosa was back at Junior School, sitting knee to knee with Sophie. Drinking from the same straw, eating yogurt from the same spoon, plaiting hair and sharing secrets. Disarmed, she dropped the books on the nearest table. 'O.K. Swapsies.'

'Mmmm,' sighed Sophie ten minutes later, licking mayonnaise from her fingers. 'I wish Mum'd buy my sandwiches from the delicatessen. They always taste better than home-made ones.'

'Oh, I don't get deli stuff every day; only when she's been to the gym next door for her work-out.'

'Work-out? You wouldn't catch my mum doing that – or me, come to think of it. Do you remember, we used to call your mum road-runner because she never stopped? Is she still like that?'

'Meep meep,' said Rosa.

Sophie giggled, then said, 'What are you going to tell her, about your skirt?' Her eyes flicked to Rosa's face, then away.

'Oh, she's got her in-service post-graduate group tonight. I'll have it washed and dry before she's home. Anyway, it's no big deal, even if she saw it. I'd just tell her I fell over on the grass.'

'Is – is that what happened, then?'

Rosa turned so that she and Sophie were face to face across the desk, knees touching. 'No,' she said.

Sophie's eyes grew wide. 'Then what . . . ?'

'It was D-cup. Andrew Greenwood. He got hold of me at break. Tried to snap off my fingers, pushed me over, that sort of stuff. . . .'

'Oh, Rosa, you poor thing. That toad! Somebody ought to sort him out. Why did he pick on you?'

'Because –' Rosa stopped and stared at Sophie. Sophie waited, her plump face flushed with anger and her green eyes flashing. ' – because – '

It was a bleak moment for Rosa. She looked at her friend and realized that she had gone beyond the warmth and ease of shared lunch-times, where secrets were swapped as freely as sandwiches. She couldn't tell the truth. She wanted to tell the truth but the words refused to come out of her mouth. The amazed delight on Sophie's face when she discovered that Rosa had fallen for Jason just like the rest of them would be too much to bear. And Sophie would tell the others. And they would say. . . .

It doesn't matter what they say, thought Rosa. It doesn't matter to me! But it did matter. She dropped her gaze to her empty lunchbox and faced the fact that it mattered very much what the others thought of her. The cool, clever image, once just a side-effect of her determination to live up to her mum's expectations, was now a part of her. It was grafted on like an extra layer of skin and she could not take it off. Rosa felt very lonely.

'– because I got in his way,' she finished.

Sophie frowned, trying to understand. Then her face cleared. 'Oh, I see!' she said. 'You don't want to boast, but I can guess what happened. There was someone else, wasn't there? D-cup was bullying some little kid and you told him to stop so he turned on you instead!'

Rosa said nothing.

'I knew it! God, Rosa, you put the rest of us to shame, the way you always wade in and say exactly what you think. You're so sure of yourself! They all admire you for it, you know. OK, so they call you Red Rosa and joke about your badges and stuff, but, well, at least we always know where we are with you.'

Rosa scowled, horribly ashamed. Sophie chatted on, but it was as though a glass screen had been drawn across the table, dividing them. Rosa stared miserably. I'm on my own, she thought. She wouldn't understand, even if I told her. No-one would, unless. . . . Unless they were going through it too. Like Meena.

'Meena! Meena, hang on!'

Meena turned, giving a puzzled frown when she saw Rosa. She waited, letting the home-time crowds surge past her, until Rosa caught up.

'Can I walk with you? I want to ask you something.'

This time Meena gave a suspicious frown, followed by a quick, tense little nod. Her long, black hair rippled like oil, then settled back in the same

38

perfect fall to her shoulder blades, where it was cut as straight as a paintbrush. They walked on down Seaton Road together, trapped in an edgy silence. Rosa cursed herself for not planning what to say. She had spent the afternoon watching the slow classroom clocks and daring to think she might have found an ally. Now, faced with Meena, all her brave dreams vanished. What if she was wrong?

'Um . . . how do you like the fourth year, then?' Rosa stalled, almost jogging to keep up with Meena's long strides.

Meena slid her a sideways glance. 'Fine,' she said, and turned her dark eyes back to the pavement ahead.

'Good. Good. Are you running for the school again this year?'

'Yes.'

'Great. Are you off to the track now?'

'Yes.'

'Look. . . . I saw you giving Andrew Greenwood that carrier bag,' Rosa blurted. 'I know what's going on.'

Meena stopped so quickly, Rosa was four steps ahead before she could slow down enough to turn back. Meena's face had turned a muddy grey and she was struggling to breathe, as though Rosa had punched her in the stomach.

'I can't,' she choked. 'Not for two of you. They'd notice if I took any more. You'll – you'll have to share his stuff.'

'Oh, no,' Rosa said, taking a step towards her. 'You've got it wrong – '

But Meena gave a wail and raced off down the street, not caring who she bumped into. For a few seconds, Rosa stared stupidly at the briefcase Meena had dropped, then she grabbed it by the handle and waved it in the air.

'Meena, wait!' she shrieked, running after her. 'Wait! You've got it all wrong! And you've left your briefcase!'

Across the street one of a gang of Year Eleven boys turned to watch. 'Whoah! Paki-hunt!' he howled. An instant later, they were all running along the opposite pavement chanting, 'Paki-hunt! Paki-hunt!'

Up ahead, Meena slowed, turned and began to walk back, her movements suddenly smooth and controlled. Rosa panted up to her and she reached out for her briefcase without looking up. Rosa held on tight.

'Give it to me!' hissed Meena. 'And don't try to stop me again, or they might decide to help you. They're just waiting for an excuse.'

Rosa looked over at the gang, who were gathered in a clump on the opposite kerb, still chanting. 'OK,' she said, 'But just listen for one minute. I'm not trying to blackmail you, Meena. Honestly. When I said I knew what was going on, I meant – it's happening to me too.'

That got a reaction. Her head snapped up and her eyes, full of tears and surprise, stared into Rosa's. Rosa nodded and said, 'I just want to help.'

Meena stared for a second longer, then she glanced over at the gang. As soon as she turned her head their way, the chanting grew louder. 'Go home, Paki! Go home, Paki!'

When Meena looked back to Rosa, her eyes were cold. 'You?' she said, 'Help me?' She tossed her head at the cluster of badges on Rosa's lapel. 'What are you after, an "I saved an Asian" badge to add to your collection? That'd really add to your right-on Leftie image.' Rosa couldn't look at her any more. She let go of the briefcase and Meena walked off.

The gang broke into a frenzy of chanting and Rosa turned on them, suddenly furious.

'Shut up!' she screamed, and they did. She filled her lungs, and carried on. 'God, you're so stupid! It really is amazing how stupid you are – it must be some sort of a record! Never mind. If you're all very good, Santa might bring you some brains this Christmas!'

Rosa ran out of breath and it dawned on her that she was the stupid one. There were four of them and they were big. The one who had started the chant stepped off the kerb and began to cross the street. He was wearing three school ties. One was knotted round his head like a sweat-band and one was tied around each bicep. Rosa's hand flew to her own school tie and he grinned. She swallowed and took a step back.

'Come on!' hissed Meena, grabbing Rosa's arm and nearly tugging her off her feet. 'Run!'

They had a good start and Rosa thought they were going to make it until she saw what was ahead. The whole pavement was blocked by a crowd which was trying to squeeze through the closing doors of an already packed school bus. 'Stand back and wait for the next one!' yelled the student teacher on bus duty, but nobody listened. Rosa felt the strength leave her legs and she slowed down, ready to give up. A roar went up behind them.

'Don't stop!' screamed Meena. She grabbed Rosa's coat and dragged her through a gate on to someone's little square of front lawn. Two more strides and they hurdled a low box hedge into the next garden, then they were over a wall and back on to the pavement, leaving the bus crowd behind them.

Seconds later, Rosa heard the thud of boots as their pursuers cleared the wall. They were getting closer. She put on a desperate spurt, but her lungs were beginning to burn.

'I can't –' she gasped. Meena glanced back once, twice, then shouted, 'Over the road. Now!'

She swerved and Rosa followed blindly, right under the wheels of the school bus. The horn blared out as she leapt for the opposite kerb and a rush of air pushed at her back like a large hand. The bus rumbled past, followed by a long tail of cars that had grown behind it while it loaded up. The gang was left on the other side of the road, looking for a space to cross.

'Very clever,' gasped Rosa, her stomach still lurching with the shock. 'Insanely stupid, but clever.'

Meena nodded. 'Come on, before the traffic clears.' She started jogging down Seaton Road.

'I can't run much further,' Rosa panted.

'We don't run. We hide,' Meena said, and turned down a side road. A screech of brakes made Rosa look back. School-tie had grown tired of waiting and stepped out in front of a car. He leaned on the bonnet, smiling in at the driver, while the other three ran through the gap he had created. Rosa gave a yelp and caught up to Meena. 'It's no good. They saw us.'

'They won't see this, though,' said Meena, and she turned smart right into an alleyway.

Rosa scurried after her but came to an abrupt stop when she saw the high wall ahead. 'Dead-end, stupid!' she hissed. Meena ignored her and tried the latch on the first of a row of wooden doors that led to the back yards of the Seaton Road terraced houses.

'Locked,' she muttered. The second latch lifted but a low, menacing growl started as soon as the hinges squeaked. Meena eased it shut again and hurried to the next gate.

'Quick! Quick!' Rosa begged, crowding up against her. The gate opened smoothly and they tumbled into the yard just as four pairs of boots thundered past the end of the alleyway.

Meena pushed the gate shut and gently lowered the latch. Then she slumped back against the wall, took a deep breath and blew her fringe out of her eyes. 'You wally,' she sighed. 'Don't you know anything? How have you managed to live this long?'

'Hey! That's not fair. I couldn't let them get away with shouting those things at you. I was trying to be supportive.'

'I could do without that sort of support.'

'But – '

'Look, the worst thing you can do is shout back: it only encourages them.' Meena shook her head. 'I would've been away and free if you hadn't started in on them.'

'I didn't ask you to come back,' snapped Rosa.

'Rosa, they would've mashed you up.'

43

'Yeah, maybe. Thanks.'

Meena gave one of the quick, dismissive nods that Rosa was getting used to. 'It looks like there's no-one home,' she said, studying the dark, empty windows of the house. 'We'd better stay here for a little while, in case they're still hanging around out there.'

'That suits me,' said Rosa, taking a deep breath, 'There's still something I want to talk about.'

Meena scowled. 'Well I don't want to talk about it, so you can just forget it, OK?'

'But Meena – '

'I said forget it!' Meena turned her back and began scraping moss from the wall with her thumbnail.

'But we can't just let him get away with it – '

'Can't we? You must be new to this, or you'd have realized that there's nothing you can do.'

'Why? How long have you been – how long has he been – '

'Blackmailing me? About eight months.' Her voice sounded calm but moss was flying off the wall in chunks.

'Eight. . . . ? But that's terrible.'

'Oh, you can get used to anything, given time,' said Meena. 'I mean, I've had kids like those – those – '

'Mutants?' Rosa suggested.

'OK,' smiled Meena, abandoning the battle with the moss and brushing her hands clean. 'I've had kids like those mutants chasing me for as long as I can remember. You get used to it. You have to.'

'But you didn't just stand there and let them

catch you! You beat them. Why won't you try to beat D-cup?'

'Look,' sighed Meena. 'My father says boys like the mutants are mostly just stupid and bored. They get their kicks out of frightening and hurting anyone different to them, it doesn't matter who. They've probably forgotten all about us by now. They'll be off tying some poor kid to a lamppost with his trousers. The chase with us, it's over. Do you see?'

'It wouldn't be like that with Andrew Greenwood. And not only because he knows – things – about us. He wouldn't. . . .' Meena hesitated, then made her hands into talons and snapped them shut. 'He wouldn't let go. He loves what he's doing to us – he feeds off it.'

A shiver juddered along Rosa's backbone like a stick dragged across railings. 'Oh, come on,' she said, trying to turn it into a shrug. 'He's just a fat slob who enjoys tormenting people.'

Meena was shaking her head vigorously. 'No, he's evil. There's something about him – he can make people do what he wants. He's turned me into a . . . a . . . thief. Every month I have to steal from my father's warehouse to keep him supplied with booze and cigarettes. Every month. And I hate it! Oh, oh how I hate it!'

'Shhhh! Don't scream like that,' hissed Rosa, flapping her arms. 'Don't get into a state – '

'What!' shrieked Meena. The dog in the next yard began to growl and scrabble at the wall.

'Please . . .' Rosa whispered, throwing a glance up at the top windows of the neighbouring houses.

Meena closed her eyes, wrapped her arms around herself and took a few deep breaths. When she opened her eyes again, she was calm. 'You haven't been listening to me,' she said, with only a slight tremble in her voice. 'Of course I'm in a state. That's what I'm trying to tell you. He's an expert at getting me into a state. He's got a lot of nasty tricks and a dreadful temper and I can't fight him because if he told everyone about the – ' Meena slapped a hand over her mouth and her eyes grew big as she realized what she had nearly said. She turned to the gate and reached for the latch.

'Meena. . . . Meena wait! Look. I'm not interested in what you did. Honestly. All I know is that when I saw you with him I was so pleased because I wasn't the only one. I – I thought we could help one another. I mean. . . .' Rosa tailed off miserably and waited for Meena to stare with cold eyes and talk about badges again.

'How? How can we help one another?' asked Meena, with her hand poised on the latch of the gate.

'There must be more of us,' Rosa said, with as much confidence as she could muster. 'He seems so – good at it. As though he's had lots of practice. And you're right, he enjoys it.'

'So, what's your plan?'

'Um . . . I haven't got as far as that. Why don't we at least try to watch him for a few days and see whether he leads us to anyone else? We could meet again on. . . . let's say Friday lunch-time in that little copse behind the music block. Please, Meena?'

Meena turned and looked at her for a few seconds, trying to decide. 'I think I have seen one other,' she said quietly.

'Oh, wow! I knew it! Who is she? Can you bring her to the meeting? Who is – '

'Don't. Don't push me. I must think about this.'

'All right,' Rosa said, forcing her voice to be calm and neutral. 'Shall I see you on Friday?'

Rosa held her breath. Again Meena hesitated. Then she gave another of her quick nods and slipped out of the gate.

O.K. Meena, twenty circuits for this session. Easy. No problem. Find your stride. Nice, gentle pace. . . . relax the shoulders. Get the breathing. Great. Good breeze tonight. Not too strong. Cool. . . . think cool. . . .

. . . . She's not like I thought she was, that Rosa Morgan. Nicer. She always looks as though she knows exactly where she's going. No doubts. But she must have slipped up somewhere along the way for him to get his claws into her. No, don't think about him. He's not allowed at the track –

– Come on, you're losing it. Watch the breathing. Lengthen the stride. Smooth. . . . smooth. . . .

I wonder what she thought of me? I wasn't very nice to her. Especially that 'I saved an Asian' rubbish, and her standing there with all her anti-apartheid and 'one world – one family' badges on. . . . oh come on, don't get the giggles in the middle of training. . . .

I feel bad about treating her like that; calling her a poser when she's so serious about her causes. It was the shock. And those mutants. She was brave, standing up to them like that. She's brave wanting to fight the other thing as well. Braver than me. She'd make a good ally and this could be my only chance to stop it. I can't do anything on my own, except more stealing. . . . more shame. . . . I can't face that much longer.

I'm going to take the chance. We. We are. That's decided. How do I feel? Like I could run for ever. Sun on my back. Power in my legs. Watch out, here comes Meena!

4

Developments

'So, is it blackmail, Rosa?'

The question sliced through her thoughts like a laser. Rosa turned from the window, rigid with shock. Mr Jackson was standing at the front of the class with a mild, questioning look on his face. Automatically, she opened her mouth to answer the teacher, but no sound came out.

'Blip . . . blip . . . blip . . . Earth to Rosa . . . Earth to Rosa . . . .' called Natalie, from the back. Rosa barely heard the giggles through the roaring in her ears. *He knows oh God they know they know. . . .*

'In the play, Rosa,' added Mr Jackson, taking pity. 'What the Joe character does to Betty; would you call it blackmail?'

Relief stormed through her. She sagged in her chair and trapped her shaking hands under the desk.

'Honestly, Sir,' sighed Natalie, 'I don't know what's got into Rosa. You're the third teacher to tell her off today. If her mother knew what – '

'That's enough, thank you, Natalie. Well, Rosa?'

'Sorry, Sir. I – I thought you said – I didn't hear the question.'

'The real question, Rosa Morgan, is why you are staring down at the Old House yard while the rest of us attempt to grapple with this GCSE set play. Hmmm? Now let's have a bit of attention, please.'

'Sir,' muttered Rosa, bending her head to the book. Her cheeks burned. She had spent the best part of two days staring out of windows and peering round corners and her hopes of finding someone else to take to the meeting were fading fast. Meena was not going to be pleased. If Meena even bothered to turn up. Rosa sighed and bent her head even further, glaring at the print so hard it began to quiver. She nearly missed the figure crossing the yard to the green painted door. It was the sudden wedge of light which drew her eye. The door was already swinging shut when she looked down but, just before it closed, Rosa caught a glimpse of a black T-shirt sleeve stretched tight across a meaty arm.

D-cup!

Rosa drew a sharp breath at the sight of him and felt the skin on her arms shiver into goose pimples. She shuddered, then became still as a thought struck her. She looked at her watch. Five minutes before the afternoon break. . . . Rosa smiled and settled back in her chair.

It was a full ten minutes into break before the girl walked into the Old House yard. Up in the empty English classroom Rosa jumped, even though she had been expecting someone. She raised her head a little more above the window-sill and peered out between two tired-looking pot plants.

'Christine Morris,' she breathed, watching the

heavy-set figure trudge over to the green painted door. The girl knocked and lifted her head for a moment, letting the lank, pale hair flop away from her face. When the door opened, her head dropped again and the hair came forward like a curtain. Rosa ducked further behind the pot plants as Andrew stared out from the doorway, checking all the Old House windows. Satisfied, he leaned against the door jamb and held out his hand. The girl scrabbled in her bag and handed over a long, white envelope. When she turned to go, Andrew grabbed her hair, spinning her back to face him. Crouched at the window, Rosa clenched her fists, trembling with anger, but the girl made no protest. She stood passively, head bowed, while he made a great show of opening the envelope and pulling out the two pink oblongs of card inside. Then he nodded and slammed the door in her face. The girl simply turned and walked away, head down. Not a word had been said.

Rosa slid down to the floor of the empty class-room and rested her back against the cold radiator. She had five minutes to work something out before the final lesson of the day. She closed her eyes and concentrated.

Christine Morris. They call her Chrissie. Year Eleven. She arrived at the beginning of term, like Jason Hughes, but without the fuss. What else? They moved here because of her dad's work. He's. . . . now what did Natalie say he was? . . . the manager of the new multi-screen complex on the edge of town –

– Cinema tickets! Oh, yes! The pink cards in the envelope she gave D-cup – complimentary tickets.

51

I wonder what she's done? No, don't think about that. Now, I've got to talk to her before tomorrow's meeting, but I don't know where she lives or anything. I'll have to wait by the Year Eleven lockers at the end of school; I'm bound to see her if I'm there quick enough. OK.

Rosa opened her eyes and grinned, finally letting her excitement take over. 'We're going to get you, D-cup, just you wait. We're going to get together and then we're going to get you!'

'Come to a meeting? Oh, no. I couldn't do that.'

'Why not?'

'Well, I wouldn't want to upset him.'

Rosa stared at the girl stolidly taking books from her locker and packing them in her bag. 'Christine – Chrissie . . . you're the one who should be upset. D-cup is blackmailing you. I saw the way he grabbed you by the hair at break. Aren't you angry?' She moved closer, trying to meet Chrissie's eyes, but Chrissie was peering intently into her empty locker, blinkered by rat tails of hair.

Rosa swore and let herself fall back against the wall of metal. The hollow clang reverberated through the lockers and grumbled away along the empty corridors of C block. She folded her arms and watched as Chrissie started to unpack the bag she had just filled, stacking text books neatly in her locker again. 'What's this?' she asked, wanting to be cruel, 'Musical books?'

A book dropped to the floor and Chrissie swung round, her blue eyes pleading. 'I don't want any trouble. I – '

'But you – we – are in trouble already! Plenty of

trouble and Andrew Greenwood is the cause of it. You can't just go on handing over cinema tickets whenever he asks for them.'

'Oh, I don't mind that. I never use them. I can't go out . . . I – I mean I don't, I don't go out much.'

Rosa bit her lip to stop herself from swearing again. 'Look,' she said, and hesitated, at a loss what to say next. Arguing with Chrissie was like wrestling with a jelly; she couldn't get a hand-hold. 'Look. . . . the tickets aren't the point here. The point is, you know, self-respect and all that. He shouldn't be allowed to treat other human beings like he's treating us. It's wrong. You should be angry. . . .'

'Should I?'

'Yes! Come to the meeting tomorrow, Chrissie.'

'Well, if you think I should . . . .'

'Great! I'll see you there,' said Rosa, turning towards the door of C-block. An instant later she ducked to the floor, pulling Chrissie with her. 'Shhhh! D-cup – walking past. . . .' Slowly, she raised her head to window level. 'He's heading for the Old House, and he's got that damned camera with him – wait a minute . . . .'

Rosa crouched down again and stared intently at the floor. 'Why didn't I think of this before? Him and that camera, in the Old House. . . . I was just a lucky bonus for him, wasn't I? He was up to something else when he found me there. He was going somewhere with that camera. . . .'

'I don't understand – ' whispered Chrissie.

'Never mind. Come on. We've got to find out what he's doing in the Old House.'

'But – I don't want any trouble – '

'Come on, Chrissie! There won't be trouble. He

went in the front door. We'll creep in the back way, through the main hall.'

The entrance hall was quiet. The setting sun was still touching the stained glass skylight at the top of the stairwell, dappling the oak floor with soft smudges of colour. Rosa took two steps into the hall and peered up at the shadowy galleries on the higher floors. Nothing moved. The stair lions glared.

They both jumped when a brief, metallic hiss broke the silence, then Rosa jumped again when Chrissie clamped a hand around her wrist, squeezing with the strength of panic. The noise had been close but muffled. He must be behind one of the heavy oak doors on the ground floor. Rosa swivelled her head, listening.

The hiss came a second time and Rosa suddenly knew it as the sliding of a filing cabinet drawer. 'School office,' she mouthed to Chrissie. 'Come on.'

She glided over to the door marked 'Reception' and Chrissie shuffled alongside, shaking her head all the while but still attached to Rosa's wrist like a handcuff. The heavy old door opened soundlessly and they eased into the tiny room that was little more than a partitioned corner of the main office.

The frosted glass reception window was not quite shut. Rosa edged forward and peered through the gap. Andrew was so close, she could have reached through the window and touched him. He was leaning over a desk, shuffling through the papers in an open file. He did not look happy.

'Nothing,' he muttered, turning back to the first page. 'Bloody nothing.' He raised the camera and photographed the page, then he slammed shut the file and stood waiting for the polaroid shot to develop. Rosa squinted down at the large black letters running along the edge of the file cover. Rosa Elizabeth Morgan.

He was looking through her school records! Her own, personal, private school records. How dare he! Rosa watched, jaw clenched, as he carried the file back to the cabinet, slid the drawer shut and locked it with a key from his pocket. She leaned slightly to get a better view through the narrow opening and her elbow touched the black bell-press on the corner of the window ledge.

The bell did not even buzz. It gave the slightest whisper of a wheeze and was silent, but Andrew heard. He swung round from the filing cabinet and stared at the frosted glass window. His eyes narrowed.

Hastily, Rosa stepped back from the crack. 'Quick!' she hissed to Chrissie. She headed for the door but was jerked to a halt after two steps. Chrissie's hand was still clamped to her wrist and Chrissie was standing rigidly to attention, staring wide-eyed at the reception window.

'No trouble,' whimpered Chrissie. 'I didn't want any trouble.'

Rosa stared up at the clock above the reception window and saw how slowly the long black second hand moved. She stared at the window glass and saw every smeary fingerprint. She stared down at Chrissie's hand and saw each chewed nail and shredded cuticle. She began to pull away from the hand with all her strength, twisting her wrist until the skin burned, but Chrissie was cold stone. The frosted glass darkened as Andrew loomed closer. His hand reached out and rested on the glass, making the window rattle in its grooves. The crack widened as the window began to slide open.

'Margaret,' called Mr Carshaw, walking from his room into the main office through the connecting door. 'Can you do one quick letter before you go? Oh, hello Andrew.'

In one smooth movement, Andrew left the window, picked up a waste bin and swept his camera into it from the desk. Then he picked up a second bin and dumped its contents over the camera. 'Evening, Sir. You just missed Mrs Watson, Sir.'

Rosa, silently prising Chrissie's cold fingers from her wrist, watched through the gap as the Headteacher frowned and walked towards Andrew, checking the room. 'But I thought I heard her at the filing cabinets . . . Why are you in here, Andrew?'

'Helping my dad, Sir. It gives me something useful to do, since I can't find a job, Sir. I can't stand to do nothing, Sir. It's a pity I didn't feel like that when I was at school, hey, Sir?' Andrew's voice was friendly, inviting laughter.

'Yes, yes,' murmured Mr Carshaw. He pulled at each of the locked cabinet drawers and looked round the room once more before giving an uncertain smile. 'Where is your dad?'

'Oh, he's around. He'll be back in a sec. I like your new car, Sir, but I couldn't help noticing that the windscreen needs a clean. Want me to do it for you, while it's parked out front there?' Andrew had managed to edge the Headteacher right back to the door of his room as he talked.

'Why, thank you, Andrew. Um. Good lad . . .'

'Come on, quickly, while they're still talking,' whispered Rosa. She took Chrissie's now unresisting arm and guided her out to the Old House entrance hall. Gingerly, they retraced their steps across the wooden floor until they reached the glass-sided corridor that linked the Old House to the main school hall. Then Chrissie broke into a clattering run and Rosa matched her speed. Suddenly caught by the universal terror of being the one at the back, they were still shoulder to shoulder when they smashed open the double doors to the main hall and carried on running, leaving the doors flapping into silence behind them.

At lunchtime the next day, Rosa waited in the sparse shelter of a leafless willow tree. A cold October rain was falling and the copse was dripping. Her shoes were waterlogged and she had discovered that her new, black winter jacket smelled like a wet dog when it got damp, but Rosa was too excited to care. At the lockers that morning, Meena had answered her questioning look with a nod and a thumbs-up sign, which could only mean that she had made a contact. Rosa could hardly wait. A break-time brush with Natalie Cooke was still fresh in her mind and she was more determined than ever to get that photograph back. Natalie would be merciless if she found out.

Any time now, thought Rosa, they'll come walking round the back of that music block and then we'll be four. She turned and grinned at Chrissie, but Chrissie was huddled against the willow trunk, head down, shoulders stooped. At least she turned up, thought Rosa, resisting an impulse to reach out and clear the wet hair from her face.

'You know, Chrissie, seeing D-cup going through my file last night gave me an idea,' said Rosa. 'A way to stop him.'

'Oh,' said Chrissie, warily. 'Good.'

Rosa sighed. 'I'll tell you when we're all here,' she said, turning back to watch for Meena. She held her plan in her mind, turning it this way and that, taking pleasure in its shimmering clarity, until Meena appeared round the corner of the music block.

'Here they come,' she crowed. 'Here they – '

Rosa stopped. Horrified, she stared out through the drooping cage of willow branches and felt her plan shatter into tiny pieces. Meena walked into the copse and behind her, his golden hair glimmering beneath the dripping trees, strolled Jason Hughes.

5

The Gatecrasher

'It's just a bunch of girls!' said Jason, pulling aside the willow branch curtain and shaking coin-sized drops of water from the leaves.

'Get in here, before someone sees you,' hissed Rosa, seething, 'and stop soaking everybody!'

'Everybody? I count three. Three girls.' Jason sniffed, pulled a face and frowned in the direction of Rosa's black jacket. 'What's that smell?'

'I count four,' snapped Rosa, wishing she and her jacket were both miles away. 'Three girls and a sexist half-wit.'

Jason stopped sniffing and looked at her properly. A lazy smile spread across his face and Rosa felt her unruly body lean towards him like a plant to light.

'Ah, yes,' he said. 'I've heard about you. You're Rosa Morgan, the one who doesn't like me. Never even met me, but you hate my guts, yes? Nice.' He dumped his school bag at the foot of the tree, sat down on it and, without seeming to try, became the centre of the group.

My meeting! thought Rosa, furiously. My idea! He can't just sit down and take over! I'll sit down as well. No, that would look as though I was being friendly.

Yes, oh yes, be friendly. Sit down and brush those raindrops out of his hair . . . .

Stop it! I feel like – like one of his handmaidens just standing here, but if I move, the smell from this stupid jacket'll waft about. Who does he think he is, taking over?

'I can't help it,' said Jason, grinning up at her.

'What . . . ?'

'Being male, or filthy rich, or incredibly good-looking – whatever it is you think you don't like me for – I can't help it. I was born that way. So stop glaring and give me a smile.' He winked one blue eye, waiting for her to melt. Expecting it.

'You big-headed . . . Why don't you just go away? This is one bunch of girls who could do without you taking over – '

'Lighten up, Rosa,' said Meena, as Jason scrambled to his feet. 'He was only joking. Sending up his image . . . you know.'

'Forget it Meena,' said Jason, shouldering his school bag. 'I think I'd better leave.'

'Oh, that's right,' shouted Rosa. 'Put me in the wrong now! Well, don't you bother to leave. I'll go. Then you three can settle down to a nice cosy chat.' Miserably, she turned away.

'Um, actually, I think I'll go too,' ventured Chrissie to the tree trunk. 'This place is out of bounds and someone might come. I – I don't want any trouble.'

'You can all stop right here,' ordered Meena in a voice that would make a charging bull elephant think again. They stopped. 'Andrew Greenwood.

D-cup. Remember him? He's the one you should be fighting. Remember? Now just you listen.

'I want you to know that it doesn't get any better. It gets worse. He won't grow tired of you. He won't stop. The stuff he's taking from you, that's only part of it. The other part, the big part, the slimy, hidden part, is that he gets a real kick out of hurting you. Like a cat with a bird. Whenever he sees you, he'll get an itch to use his claws.

'Trying to keep out of his way will rule your lives. You'll spend your days at school looking over your shoulders and walking close up against the wall in corridors, hoping he won't see you. You'll stop going to after-school clubs because he's around. You'll stop playing tennis because the courts are next to the caretaker's bungalow. You'll stop using the new school sports centre because he likes to watch the girls in the pool, and you'll miss out on the school discos for the same reason. He'll find you, though.

'You'll be sitting in the sun, checking through your history homework before the lesson and he'll come up behind you and he'll snatch it out of your hand and he'll tear it up and screw it up and throw it in the bin. He'll say, "Help your caretaker, help your school. Put your rubbish in the bin."

'Or he'll meet you at the school gates one morning and make you run all the way back to the post box with a letter. You'll be late for school but you're glad he let you off so lightly. Then he'll tell you that the letter was to the *Evening Telegraph*. He'll tell you that he had a sudden urge to let people know the truth and he thinks you ought to keep an eye on the personal columns and you're so scared for the rest of the week and you buy the paper and you look and you look and there's nothing.

'Or he'll find you in the yard and put his arm around you in front of everyone and walk you along, smiling and friendly, but his fingers will be digging into your shoulder and he'll be telling you that he thinks you're the lowest form of life and he's going to come round to your house and have a good look at your parents to see what could produce such a creature . . . .'

Meena's voice cracked and she came to a halt. They all let out the breath they had been holding in a collective sigh but Meena hadn't finished. She cleared her throat once, twice, and carried on.

'Running kept me going. Running and the track. I wouldn't let him into my head at the track. I was managing. And then you came along, Rosa, and you said you wanted to help. Eight months of hanging on and managing, then you came along and told me only a coward would put up with it – '

'I didn't say that,' protested Rosa.

'Not exactly, but you thought it.'

Raindrops pattered on leaves. Chrissie swallowed with a painful click. 'I'm sorry, Meena,' said Rosa, looking down at her wet shoes. 'I didn't know how bad it had been – '

'I know you didn't. None of you know – how can you? He hasn't had you for long enough. What is it? A few weeks?'

'Five days,' muttered Rosa.

Meena turned to Jason. 'Five weeks,' he said quietly.

'Um, six. Six weeks,' whispered Chrissie.

Meena nodded. 'The worst bit is how you feel

about yourself,' she said. 'You feel – dirty. Grubby. There's no joy. And you are alone. It's as though everyone else is on the other side of a fence, a high, wire-mesh fence. You can see them living their lives; you can walk alongside them; you can even talk to them, but you are alone. You know, I was so excited when Rosa set up this meeting. I thought, even if we can't fix D-cup, at least we'll be together. At least I won't be alone behind the fence.'

Meena's voice was shaking now. Her whole body was shivering and her head was wobbling on her neck, ticking out little nods in time with the beat of her heart. 'A-and now you're going . . . I – I – don't – I . . . .'

Rose stood, appalled, and watched Meena shake. She was still trying to work out the best thing to do when Jason dropped his bag and wrapped his arms around Meena.

Yes, of course, that's the best thing to do, thought Rosa and felt inadequate and wished fiercely that Jason was hugging her, all in one lurching second.

'Don't worry, Meena, we'll fix D-cup, won't we?' said Jason. He looked at Chrissie over Meena's head.

'Um, yes,' said Chrissie, obediently, and was rewarded with a dazzling smile.

'We'll meet up at my place, seven o'clock tonight, and figure out a plan. I'll send out for some pizzas, OK?'

'Make it seven-thirty,' said Meena, emerging from under his jacket. 'I've got training.'

'Oh, yeah! Now that's what I call tough!' crowed Jason and Meena produced a tiny smile. 'Seven-thirty it is. Come in through the side gate and head for the shed at the end of the garden. It's sort of my private den. OK, Rosa?' he added carefully, finally turning to include her.

Rosa stared at the three of them – Jason, Meena and Chrissie – all looking at her expectantly. Her face was blank but inside she was panicking. If she said yes, she could be near him again and part of her yearned to be near him, even as she wished Meena had never brought him. If she said no, the group would meet anyway, and she would be alone.

But I've got to say no. I've got to! He's the reason I'm in this mess to start with. If anyone found out I was going to his house after everything I've said . . . Rosa closed her eyes, picturing Sophie's shocked face, Natalie's triumphant grin. Or if he found out why D-cup was blackmailing me . . . .

Rosa opened her eyes, then opened her mouth to say no. 'I'll be there,' she said, and clamped her lips together, astonished. Immediately, the other three broke into relieved smiles. As though they really want me to be there, thought Rosa, and an answering smile spread across her face.

'Four against one,' said Meena, with quiet satisfaction.

They stood together under the willow tree, unwilling to break the bond, until a distant bell began to ring.

'Double maths,' sighed Rosa, suddenly realizing how cold and wet she was. 'We'd better leave one at a time; it's best not to be seen together. And no meetings at school from now on – too risky.'

Jason picked up a muddy twig and smeared a line of dirt across each cheekbone. 'OK, Sarge,' he said, saluting. 'We lie low. Rendezvous nineteen-

64

thirty hours. Keep me covered.' He zig-zagged through the copse, stopping to flatten himself against the wall of the music block before disappearing round the corner.

'Doesn't he take anything seriously?' sighed Rosa, trying to ignore a perverse pang of loss and longing.

'Give him a break,' said Meena. 'He's taking it seriously. That's just his way. See you later.'

Meena strode off and Chrissie scurried after her. Rosa brought up the rear, sniffing at her jacket sleeve, trying to decide whether to stuff it in her locker and face a wet coat at the end of the day or to let it steam doggily against the maths room radiator.

Only when the copse was empty did the figure step out of the shadows at the back of the dark practice room. He kicked aside a tangle of music stands to reach the window overlooking the willow tree. His skull earring shone dully in the grey light and his breath fogged the pane. He drew a stick girl in the condensation on the glass. He gave the stick girl lots of long, curly hair. Then he drew a dagger, stabbing into her side. He watched condensation drip from the point of the dagger and his smile was the cold, hungry smile of a hunting shark.

Rosa was late. She had meant to be late, to avoid being alone with Jason, but not this late. She had forgotten how long and winding Stoneleigh Avenue was. The big houses stretched out luxuriously along its length, each wrapped in space and privacy.

The walking was easy. The pavements here were smooth and wide, with mature trees spaced along the neatly cut grass verges. Every street light was working. Even the rain fell in an orderly fashion. Unable to find a single pothole to fill, it trickled meekly into the gutter and poured itself down the drain. Rosa set her shoulders and marched on, refusing to let herself feel like an intruder. She was so busy looking for house names, she failed to notice the figure trailing her soundlessly along the grass verge, always keeping three trees back.

' "Greenacres", at last!' she muttered, turning in between stone pillars and hurrying up the driveway towards a large, white house. A security light opened its yellow eye and showed her the wrought iron gate beside the garages. She lifted the latch and went through.

A domed glass extension had been built on to the back of the house. Rosa could see water shimmering between the leaves of the potted plants inside. The legendary swimming pool, she thought, remembering the gossip about Greenacres parties. It was Natalie Cooke's sole ambition to get an invitation to a Greenacres party. If Natalie could see me now, thought Rosa.

With a sigh, she turned away from the pool and stared past lawns and flowerbeds to Jason's shed. It was easy to find. The security light behind her had clicked off but the windows of the shed glowed brightly through the rain. Shed? thought Rosa, looking more closely at the tiled roof and the covered verandah with steps and a rail. It's nearly a house!

Late as she was, Rosa stood in the rain, reluctant to move. She had to choose. Walk away now and fight Andrew alone, or face up to Jason and the way he made her feel. She screwed up her face and groaned softly.

Just then, the security light at the front of the house blinked on again, tracing the pattern of the wrought iron gate on the path and adding yellow highlights to the puddles. Oh, good, I'm not the last, thought Rosa and turned to greet Meena or Chrissie.

There was no one at the gate.

Rosa frowned. She waited a few seconds. Still no one. But something must have crossed the beam and triggered the light. Rosa grew very still and listened, mouth open. Perhaps someone had walked past the house? No, she had been at least half way up the drive before the beam was activated. Rosa swallowed. What if it was . . . No, stupid, it couldn't be him, could it . . . ? Her eyes were beginning to water but she kept staring at the gate, not daring to blink. She took one soft step backwards, then another.

When a black shape poured itself between the curls of iron, she nearly screamed. The cat turned its yellow eyes on her for a second then melted into the bushes at the back of the garages. Rosa's shoulders sagged. She let out her breath and cursed softly. Then she turned and hurried across the garden towards the shed, suddenly needing light and warmth and company. She did not hear the slight click as the latch of the gate lifted behind her.

'Who's there?' asked Jason, in answer to her knock.

'Who do you think?' hissed Rosa, hating the way her heart flipped at the sound of his voice.

67

Instantly, the shed door opened. 'Welcome,' smiled Jason.

Rosa stepped inside.

And froze.

Her breath stopped in her throat and she stared around her, deaf to the greetings of Meena and Chrissie. She was standing on a small plateau, half way up a mountainside. It was a warm, summer night; she could hear the crickets singing and smell the clean, green scent of pine needles. The stars wheeled above and a full moon hung over the mountain peak behind her. Far below the edge of the plateau, a wide plain stretched to the horizon. The sky above the horizon still glowed where the sun had set, but the plain was in darkness, pinpointed by chains and clusters of tiny lights. An owl hooted and Rosa turned to look for it. She saw instead a fox, one paw lifted, just behind the grassy bank where Chrissie sat. Its eyes were red and it was looking at her.

'Oh!' Rosa took a step back. Her foot clunked on a wooden floor, Chrissie giggled and the illusion was broken. She was in a shed with painted walls and Christmas lights strung across the roof space. The moon was a light-bulb, encased in a white glass globe.

'Isn't it lovely?' said Chrissie. 'Look!' She pulled back a handful of turf. 'It's a great big piece of green cloth with all mattresses and bean-bags underneath! He's even got a sound-effects tape.'

Rose turned to Jason. 'It's brilliant,' she said, still too stunned to be anything but honest. Jason smiled and his eyes shone in the soft lamplight. He really was beautiful. Rosa stared into his eyes and felt all her bones turn into liquorice boot laces.

'How do you do it?' she asked.

'Come here, I'll show you.'

Rosa stepped closer and realized that the scent of pine needles was coming from him. She took a deep breath.

'See?' Jason was saying. 'These walls are chipboard. I put it up to insulate the place, but it looked so bare and grey, I went out and bought loads of big sheets of white card and some cans of spray paint and . . .' He spread his arms. 'I just rip it all down and start again, when I get tired of something.'

'What, after all this work? How could you? What was here before this one, then?'

'It was the cockpit of a plane. It was great. I did all the dials with luminous paint, and through the windscreen, nothing to see but sky – ' Jason stopped then and his face, which had been alight with pleasure, darkened. ' – but I took it down five weeks ago,' he muttered, turning away. Rosa was suddenly looking at the tense, lonely profile of the boy in the Portraits photograph. Her cheeks began to burn and she glanced away, pretending to study the painting.

'Yes,' she said. 'I love the way that valley seems to – '

'Greenwood broke in here, you see,' blurted Jason, clenching his fists. 'I had to change it, once I knew he'd seen it. He m-made it – bad. Nobody comes in here. This is m-my . . . this is mine.' Jason stopped then pressed his fingers to his lips for an instant, as if to halt the stutter.

'D-cup broke in?' asked Meena. 'Here? You mean he actually came to your home?'

'Yeah. It was easy for him. There was only a padlock on the door. That Yale lock's new. I put it on afterwards.'

Rosa stared at the shiny lock and thought about her own back door, wedged shut with a block of wood since her brother lost the only key. The hairs rose on the back of her neck.

'But, surely he can't be blackmailing you over this?' said Meena. 'This painting walls, it's not shameful . . .'

'No, not this. He was after – something else.'

Nobody spoke. Something else? The words swelled and ballooned until they seemed to take all the space in the shed, but still nobody asked what Andrew had been after. They couldn't. The something else was Jason's secret and they each had a secret of their own to keep. Rosa trawled her empty head for something to say and netted another question.

'So why invite us?' she asked. 'If you don't like people coming in here?'

Jason shrugged. 'We're here to stop D-cup. It'll be like an antidote; a way to wipe out what he did to this place by breaking in. Anyway, the only other private place is my bedroom, and that doesn't belong to me like this does. My mother had it decorated the way she thought a boy's bedroom should look, but she didn't ask me first. She's like that, my m-mother.' Again, Jason stopped and briefly pressed his fingers to his lips. Rosa watched, intrigued. Shallow? Insensitive? Perhaps she had misjudged him.

With a decisive click, the crickets stopped singing. 'Right,' said Meena, tossing Jason's cassette recorder on to the bean-bag beside her. 'Let's get down to business. We've wasted enough time. And you were late, Rosa. I thought you were serious about this?'

Rosa stared at Meena. Meena, looking neat and impatient in her tracksuit and trainers, gazed back.

'Yeah,' said Jason, hurriedly. 'We've been waiting to order the pizzas for the last half an hour. Now that's serious.'

'Some of us have got younger brothers to get tea for and paper rounds to do,' snapped Rosa, turning on him instead.

He held up his hands and pretended to cringe behind them. 'OK, OK. I'll order right away. You look different out of school uniform,' he added, punching buttons on his mobile phone. 'I like the . . .' he indicated her best lycra jumpsuit. 'And those earrings . . . Great.'

Rosa suddenly felt over-dressed. She scowled, hating him for noticing the care she had taken, but Jason had turned away. 'Ciao, Giovanna,' he crooned into the 'phone and began to converse in startlingly fluent Italian. No, I was right, she thought. He's a poser.

'Close your mouth, Chrissie, and try not to look so impressed,' said Rosa, settling herself on a bean-bag. 'He probably learned the menu off by heart. Now, Meena, here's some business for us to get down to. I'll tell you what Chrissie and I saw last night.'

'The school files,' breathed Meena, when Rosa had finished. 'So that's how he found out about me.

71

But . . . how does he know which file to look in? I mean, he can't just browse through every file on the off-chance of digging up some dirt; it's risky going through those office cabinets, someone could walk in on him at any minute. Carshaw nearly did. How does he know who's got a secret to start with?'

'Perhaps he can sniff out secrets, or – or see them lurking just under a person's skin, like very faint tattoos,' said Chrissie, staring wide-eyed into space. She shuddered at her own words and tried to rub the gooseflesh from her arms.

'Thank you, Steven King, for joining us here on "After Dark," ' said Jason.

'. . . Sorry. I didn't mean to, um . . . My stupid imagination . . .' Chrissie ducked her head and shuffled backwards to her bolt-hole amongst the mattress cushions.

'No,' said Rosa softly, suddenly understanding. 'We're looking at this the wrong way. He doesn't sniff out secrets – he sniffs out people who can get things he wants. Very clever.'

'What is?'

'Don't you see, Meena? Most people have a secret if you dig deep enough. Something they really don't want others to know about. D-cup just targets someone who can get hold of booze and cigarettes, or cinema tickets, or . . . What's he getting from you, Jason?'

'Match tickets, City strip, signed footballs – '

'See? D-cup picks out people with something to offer and then he starts digging for a secret he can use against them. And sometimes, he finds one.'

Meena was nodding furiously. 'You're right! It all fits together. He didn't start blackmailing me until the middle of Year Nine, right after my family took over those off-licences, but my – secret – happened before I even started at Seaton.'

'Hang on though, Rosa. You saw him looking through your file when he'd already started blackmailing you,' said Jason.

'Yes, but I think I was a mistake. I think he was heading for the school office with that polaroid camera to check out someone else's file, when he caught me – well, doing something I wouldn't want known – ' Rosa stopped speaking as she felt a hot blush spread across her face. She found herself unable to look at Jason.

' – and he took a photograph?' prompted Jason.

Rosa nodded. 'He thought I was a lucky bonus but now he's not quite sure what to do with me. He's looked in my file and found out that my mum's a History Lecturer and my dad's a Librarian. Big deal. Nothing there he wants, you see. All he's had from me is money, and not much of that. The thing is, if he was going to look at another file when he caught me, I wonder just how many other people – '

Rosa stopped in mid-sentence as Meena jumped to her feet and turned to stare at the shed wall behind her chair.

'What – ?' Jason began but Meena whipped round and shook her head at him.

'Listen,' she mouthed and raised her arm to point a shaking finger at the side of the wall of the shed.

Chrissie gave a faint whimper, grabbed a cushion and cowered behind it. Rosa remembered the security light and her heart squeezed itself into a painful knot. They listened hard. Not moving. Not breathing.

There! A soft footfall . . .

There! The creak of a verandah board . . .

And there! A shoulder brushing against the shed wall . . .

Meena's arm ticked round like a compass arrow, marking the location of each new sound. They watched, horrified, as her finger traced a slow path from the side of the shed to the front until, at last, it was pointing straight at the unlocked door.

6
One of Us

Trapped in the depths of her bean-bag, Rosa stared at the shed door.

He's out there oh he's just outside I can hear him breathing, she thought, listening to her own blood surging in her ears.

Stay shut, she pleaded, shooting arrows of concentrated thought energy at the door as though willpower alone could stop it from opening. Stay shut. . . . stay shut. . . .

Meena was looking at the Yale lock, trying to make herself walk over and release the latch. Two steps to lock the door. Come on, two quick steps. But her feet refused to budge and she could only watch as, slowly, the door handle started to turn.

Chrissie moaned and burrowed deeper into her pile of cushions. Rose floundered from the bean-bag to her knees but was knocked backwards again when Jason pushed past.

'My place,' he said in a strange, harsh voice, as the door inched open. 'My place!' he roared, rushing forward and wrenching the door wide. Someone stumbled into the room, still hanging from the door handle. Instinctively, Meena flung up an arm to protect herself and there was a strangled cry from the intruder as her elbow crunched into his nose.

He folded up and curled into a ball on the floor. 'Don't hit me!' he whimpered. 'I wasn't doing anything, honest.'

Jason stood trembling. The tidal wave of rage which had gathered him up and swept him roaring to the door had rolled on. He was breathing hard and his face was blank as he looked down at the crumpled figure on the floor. Then the boy wiped an arm across his nose and his shirt sleeve was suddenly, joltingly, red with blood. Jason gasped and his brain started working again. 'That's not D-cup,' he said, hugely relieved.

'No. It's only Liam O'Donnell,' said Rosa, scrambling to her feet. The boy raised his head and looked at her. Blood streamed from his nose and his grey eyes were watery with pain.

'What the hell are you doing, creeping about, spying on us?' Rosa demanded, furious with him for giving them such a fright. 'You followed me here, didn't you?'

'Yes. I – '

'You little – ' Rosa took a step forward and Liam curled into a ball again, shouting, 'He made me do it! He made me do it! He made me do it!'

Meena's head came up and she stared across at the others. They returned her gaze with wordless understanding. Liam gradually became aware that his snuffling sobs were the only sounds in the room. Warily, he sat up. 'Who made you do it?' asked Meena softly, although they all knew the answer.

'D-cup.'

'You're one of us, aren't you?' said Jason. 'He's got his claws in you, too.'

Liam nodded vigorously, then winced at the starburst of pain in his nose. 'D-cup found me this afternoon and told me to watch her,' he said, pointing at Rosa. 'I didn't know why, though. He just said to follow her all week-end then tell him what she got up to. He was mad.'

'Oh, no,' groaned Rosa. 'That was so stupid, us meeting at school. D-cup must have trailed one of us to the willow tree.'

'I've been following her since the end of school and she never saw me behind her,' continued Liam, with a touch of pride. 'I was doing all right until I heard you all saying about, you know. . . . It made me want to come in here too. So I did. That's all.'

Liam stopped and stared down at his knees, with a puzzled look on his face. He never joined groups. He never talked much. Until now.

Jason knelt and gently lifted Liam's head to inspect the damaged nose. 'Not broken,' he decided, handing him a handkerchief and running a hand over the cropped dark hair that covered his head like velvet. 'You'll be all right, Mouse.'

Rosa looked down at Liam crouched on the floor. She saw how his short, furry hair left his ears showing pink and naked and how big his eyes looked in his pointy little face.

'Yes, Mouse!' she cried and Liam smiled.

'Five against one,' said Meena, grinning.

'And we've got our mystery to solve,' said Rosa, beginning to giggle. 'All we need now is a dog called Tim, some baggy shorts and a haunted castle!'

'Jolly super,' said Chrissie, catching on immediately. 'We'll jolly well trounce that scoundrel, then we'll jolly well have a scrumptious tea with lots of scones and lemonade and ice-cream and – '

'Pizzas!' called a voice from the garden.

'Ice-cream and pizzas?' said Meena, and her comical expression tipped them over into wild, whooping laughter which swirled out of the shed taking all their tension with it. The pizza boy appeared in the doorway and his jaw dropped as he saw the blood and the mountain and the wheeling stars.

'Hea-vy,' he breathed. 'What are you lot on? Ganja? Crack?'

'No, bean-bags,' spluttered Rosa and the laughter soared again.

Liam picked every anchovy, olive and sun-dried tomato from his pizza slice and arranged them in a neat pile on the box lid. Already three red, green and black waste-tips sat on the cardboard, each in the centre of a spreading olive oil slick. Satisfied, he lifted the pizza to his mouth and chewed steadily, not lowering his hands until it was gone.

'Have another slice, Mouse,' said Jason, apparently unconcerned that Liam was removing all the authentic Italian touches from his authentic Italian pizza. 'I don't supposed you've had much to eat tonight, what with working on your first stake-out.'

Rosa nestled in the hollow of her bean-bag and watched as Liam methodically built his fifth reject pile. She was still glowing with the knowledge that she, Rosa Morgan, had made them all laugh. It was a good feeling. She gazed round at the others fondly, surprised to find that for once she could look at Jason without catapulting between yearning and anger. He's just part of the group, she thought as she snuggled further into her bean-bag, feeling warm and sleepy and full of pizza. And I'm part of the group too and it's lovely because. . . .

. . . . Because I've been so lonely, cried a hurt little voice, swimming up through the cold years of struggling to be in control and clever and a credit to her mother. I never used to be so lonely, keened the voice, breaking surface. I used to have friends. I did . . .

Rosa's eyes flew open and a single tear slid from each corner into her hair. She found the locket under her jumpsuit and pressed it hard against her breast-bone until the voice sank back into silence and she was in control. But things were not quite the same. The voice had left a mournful ripple which spread through her mind, rocking all her certainties.

Swiftly, Rosa sat up and looked for something to occupy her thoughts. Liam sat opposite, still working his way through the pizza, and she concentrated on him.

He was in Year Ten at Seaton but he was small enough to be taken for a Year Eight boy. He still had the high voice of a young boy but with a rough edge to it. Smoker, thought Rosa, checking out the yellow smears on his fingers. He lived on the notorious Hilltop estate and he was the youngest of a big family. Rosa didn't know the exact number of brothers and sisters but at junior school every class seemed to have an O'Donnell in it. His mother had died when he was at junior school. Rosa still remembered the day all the O'Donnells stayed away and Miss Edwards said a prayer for them in assembly. The news had rumbled through the school like an earth tremor, showing them that even solid ground could suddenly shift. Shaken, they had rushed to the gate at the end of the day to make sure someone was waiting for them.

Liam hadn't been at school much since then. When he did turn up he was never badly behaved, just bewildered. He always brought his rucksack because everyone else carried a bag to school, but there was nothing in it. He would sit at the back while the teachers valiantly attempted to include him in the pattern their class had been weaving together all term. After a while he would quietly disappear again.

Rosa turned her attention to his clothes. Does he ever wear anything else, she thought, eyeing the greasy red, white and blue ski-jacket which only came off on the hottest days and then it was tied round his waist by the sleeves. Underneath, he wore a cheap grey nylon shirt with two buttons missing. His school trousers were shiny at the knees and too short although they had been let down twice. Rosa stared at the white lines marking earlier hems like growth rings in a tree and for the first time she understood that, for Liam, clothes had nothing to do with looking good or making a fashion statement. For Liam, clothes meant jumble-sales and hand-me-downs and never being quite warm enough in winter. He had spent his whole childhood growing into oversized bargains from market stalls, then growing out of them again.

I'll bet he's never worn a nylon shirt in his life, thought Rosa, turning her attention to Jason. Is

that what gives him charisma? Does money give
him the right to hand out nick-names? Or is it his
good looks? If I was rich and beautiful, would I
have that power too? Because I want it. I want to
be the sort of person who hands out nick-names
instead of being given one. I'm –

– jealous? Rosa shifted uncomfortably in the
bean-bag. I can't be jealous of him. I despise him,
don't I? Oh, but the way life seems to fit him just
like his clothes. . . .

'Look, if everyone's finished eating, can we get
on? My father is coming to collect me in half an
hour and we haven't decided anything yet.'

Rosa smiled at Meena, grateful for the interrup-
tion.

'First of all,' continued Meena, 'we have to work
out what Mouse is going to tell D-cup on Monday.'

'Um, I've been thinking about that,' ventured
Chrissie. 'He can't just say nothing happened. He's
got to put D-cup off the scent . . .' She hesitated,
peering out from under her hair to make sure they
liked what she was saying.

'So?' prompted Meena.

'Um, so, he could say that he followed Rosa to
Jason's house and he saw Jason slam the front door
in her face and . . . and then she ran home crying
and stayed in her house for the rest of the week-
end.' Chrissie paused for breath, glowing with the
pleasure of her invention, but her cheeks paled
again when she saw Rosa's horrified face. 'Um. . . .
so then D-cup will think that, um, the lunch-time
meeting was a wash-out, a-and – '

'Get lost, Chrissie!' yelled Rosa. 'No way!'

'Oh, dear. I only meant – '

'What Chrissie meant is that Andrew Greenwood sees you as the trouble-maker here, Rosa. If he thinks we're too frightened to listen to you and your ideas, he'll relax and carry on as normal. Isn't that right?' asked Meena.

Chrissie nodded from behind her screen of hair.

'But – ' said Rosa, and stopped. What could she say?. . . . Actually, if you tell D-cup that Jason sent me away in tears he's going to make my life hell because Jason is the reason I'm being blackmailed. . . .

' – couldn't . . . couldn't I get thrown out of someone else's house?' finished Rosa, lamely.

Jason clutched his hands to his heart and staggered. 'My life is over,' he gasped. 'If my house isn't good enough for Rosa Morgan to get thrown out of, there's no point in going on.'

He collapsed against Chrissie, sobbing into her shoulder, then he rolled off the mattress to lie at Rosa's feet. 'Please, please. Let it be my house,' he begged, grabbing her hand.

Pleasure danced along her fingers, pleasure so bright and strong that she snatched her hand from his and instantly wished it back again.

'Why do you always have to touch everyone? Touching, touching, always touching,' she snapped, seeing his arms around Meena, his hand in Liam's hair, his head on Chrissie's shoulder. 'As if we were your pet animals, or something.'

The laughter faltered and stopped. The other three looked at Jason's bewildered face and they looked at her and Rosa knew what they were seeing. The Nice Guy and the Ice Queen. She was trapped inside a Hollywood cliche but she had to play the part because the truth was even worse. 'I'm not your pet,' she finished, miserably.

'I know you're not my pet,' said Jason. 'I'd need a special licence to keep a dangerous animal.' He smiled, to show that it was a joke, but his eyes were cold.

'Anyway, it can't be anyone else's house,' said Meena, dragging them back to the main business. 'Mouse here has to be as convincing as he can, and he'll be more convincing if he's describing a place he's actually been to. All right?'

'All right, all right. It's no big deal,' sighed Rosa. 'Can we get on to the important stuff? Like how to stop D-cup?' She raised her eye-brows and looked around, relishing the silence, back in control. Three more seconds, she thought, then I'll zap them with my plan. One. . . . Two. . . .

'I've been thinking about D-cup getting off on tormenting us,' said Jason. 'Meena's right – that's why he does the whole blackmail bit. I mean, yeah, he picks on people who can get him stuff – a few cans of beer, free match tickets – but he's not exactly hitting the big-time. He might kid himself that he does it for the loot, but it's just the bait. . . . the hook to get him started. What it comes down to is he loves bullying.'

'Jason, we know he's evil,' said Rosa, anxious to get on and outline her plan. 'We're here to stop him, not sit about trying to understand him.'

'But that's how we stop him, by using his weakness! You see he could have arranged it so that he never had to meet us at all. He could have made us drop off the stuff say, once a month, in a pre-

83

arranged spot; but he has to have his face-to-face sessions – and that's how we trip him up.'

Jason scrambled to his feet and fetched a sports bag from the corner. 'We play him at his own game,' he said, reaching into the bag. 'We get evidence of D-cup blackmailing us.' He lifted out a cam-corder, then a tiny cassette recorder, and laid them on the floor. 'Once he knows we've got him on tape, he won't dare to touch us again. Stalemate.'

Meena nodded slowly. 'Not bad,' she said and Jason grinned.

'Brilliant,' whispered Chrissie. 'It's just like this book I'm reading where the detective gets wired up for a meeting with the gangland boss and makes him incriminate himself on tape.'

'What do you think, Mouse?'

Liam smiled and stretched out a finger to touch the smooth, black skin of the cam-corder. 'Sounds good,' he said.

Jason turned to Rosa. At first she was silent, although there were many things she wanted to say to him. That was my idea, she wanted to scream. I thought of it first! Why should you get the credit when you stole my plan? Instead, she glared into the depths of the cam-corder's fish-eye lense and thought about the battered cassette recorder she had been about to bring out of her bag.

'So, someone is going to stroll up to D-cup with that thing perched on one shoulder. Very subtle. What are we going to do, disguise it as a parrot?'

'No, Rosa,' explained Chrissie, earnestly. 'The one who has to see him will have the mini-cassette recorder. The cam-corder'll be somewhere else –

84

maybe in that classroom where you hid, above the Old House back yard.'

'Oh, shut up, will you?' snapped Rosa, turning all her frustration on Chrissie. 'I didn't seriously believe – oh, never mind, Chrissie. Who do you think you're kidding, anyway, sitting here planning how to beat D-cup. You love it when it's all like a great big story, but as soon as the action starts, you'll turn to jelly and start saying, "I don't want any trouble . . ." '

For a second, Chrissie's eyes met hers and Rosa saw the hurt. Then Chrissie hid behind her hair and laughed, the way she always laughed at insults. I'm not angry, said the laugh, I'm not upset! Don't anybody stick up for me, I can take a joke! Some-times, other people laughed too, and that pleased Chrissie, because Rosa was right; she hated trouble.

This time no one else laughed. Chrissie let her high-pitched shrieks go on a little too long, hoping they would join in. When she stopped, there was silence. She hung her head. Dad's right, she thought savagely, I am a doormat.

Jason stared at Rosa. 'Don't you like my idea? Is that it?' he said.

'No, it's a good idea, I think we should do it,' said Rosa, trying, unsuccessfully, to catch Chrissie's eye.

'Fine. Then we're all agreed,' said Jason. 'Now here's the difficult part. We're going to have to tell each other our secrets.'

In the stunned silence that followed, Liam got to his feet and walked to the shed door.

'Wait a minute, Mouse, please! Listen to me just for a minute, before you go . . .'

Liam pushed his hands into the pockets of his ski jacket and turned to face Jason, his back against the door.

'OK. All right. Now, just think about it. One of us is going to have to get D-cup to say, on tape, that he's a blackmailer. The chances are D-cup is going to talk about that person's secret as well. We can edit the cassette tape, that's no problem, but we'd have to listen to it first. See what I mean? We can't expect one person to give away their secret and not the others. Besides, if we all share our secrets, we'll be strong. He won't be able to play us off against each other.'

'And no-one's going to gossip,' said Meena. 'We've all got too much to lose.' She thought about telling her secret and was surprised to feel relief spread through her at the prospect.

'Look, we don't have to decide yet,' said Jason. 'Let's arrange another meeting and anyone who doesn't want to talk just stays away. If you don't turn up, you're on your own after that, though. Agreed?'

Rosa was trying to keep her face blank but inside she was horrified. I can't! I can't tell him! I'd die, she thought. But I was the one who got this group started, why should I have to leave? It's not fair! Then the answer came to her. She could lie. 'Agreed,' she said.

'We need a place to meet,' said Meena. 'Not here. D-cup knows about it, and anyone could eavesdrop.'

'My mum and dad are out next Friday evening. Why not come to my place?' suggested Chrissie, flinging back her hair and sending Rosa a defiant look.

A rush of colder air made them look to the door. Liam was just slipping out.

'Mouse?' called Jason. 'At least think about it, will you?'

The latch clicked shut.

A week later, Rosa boarded the bus that would take her to the Lakeview Estate and Chrissie's house. Jason waved from the back and she checked the other passengers before moving to sit beside him. She breathed in the scent of pine and resisted an impulse to trace the curve of his cheekbone with her finger.

'Are you all right?' he asked. 'Meena 'phoned me to say D-cup was giving you a hard time.'

'He was waiting for me at the gates on Monday morning,' said Rosa, remembering the fingernails digging into the back of her neck and the voice hissing, 'See me at break, bird-mess.'

'Was it bad?' asked Jason.

Rose couldn't look at him. She was hearing Andrew's mocking voice bouncing from the walls of the Old House yard. 'So, bird-mess, you thought you'd get me and get him all in one go, did you? But Prince Charming slammed the door in Cinderella's face, didn't he? And poor little Cinders ran home crying. That's not supposed to happen, is it? Prince Charming isn't supposed to treat Cinders like a piece of bird-mess, is he. . . ?'

'Did he hurt you?' asked Jason.

Rosa rolled up her sleeves to show the bruises. He stared, then gently touched his fingertips to the purpling skin. 'Snap,' he said lightly, rolling up his own sleeve.

'He did that to you?' asked Rosa, strangely shocked.

'Yep. He knows I daren't hit back, not with what he's got on me. Meena says you had to give him more money?'

'Another fiver. It's odd though, he doesn't seem that interested in the money. I wonder why? He said he was only taking it to teach me a lesson. He actually wagged his finger at me, like some sort of psychotic headteacher.'

Jason laughed. 'You're very witty, when you want to be,' he said.

Rosa tried to think of a witty reply. 'Thanks,' she said, finally. Then she smiled at Jason Hughes for the first time.

Meena climbed aboard at the next stop, waving goodbye to her brother. She sat down on Rosa's other side and said, 'Well done, kid. You got through it.'

'Yeah, well thanks for the 'phone calls. They really helped.'

'You looked so rough on Monday afternoon, I had to do something. Sorry I couldn't say much. Our 'phone's in the hall and Grandfather has ears like a bat.'

'Mouse must have told his story well,' said Rosa. 'D-cup swallowed the whole thing.'

'Phase one of our plan successfully completed. Oh, it feels so good to be doing something at last!' Meena hugged herself and grinned at Rosa and Jason.

'And it's half term now. We can be together for

a whole week without worrying about D-cup,' said Rosa, happily. A second later she froze, realizing what she had just said, but Jason and Meena were nodding in agreement. Rosa sat back between them and enjoyed the bus ride through the dark streets. She enjoyed the harsh lights, the hard seats and the smell like damp cardboard. She loved the way the bus whined through its nose at every hill and the way Jason leaned against her at every right turn. She was sorry when it was over.

'So, this is Lakeview Estate,' she said, as they jumped down from the bus into a road of neat, new houses. 'It's like Munchkinland.'

'What's that?' asked Meena, looking for street names.

'You know, that toytown place in The Wizard of Oz, full of silly little people busy doing nothing.'

'Good film, that,' said Jason, mildly.

'Yes, but what I mean is, these new estates – they're so. . . . twee. Look at them all trying to make their little boxes look different. See? Pointless little fake window shutters, carriage lamps, even a wishing well!'

'Hmmmm,' said Jason, his eyes on the road ahead.

'There it is,' said Meena. 'Cherry Tree Gardens.'

'Net curtains. . . .' sneered Rosa. 'Satellite dishes. . . . don't you think it's awful?'

'Doesn't matter what I think,' said Jason. 'I'm not living here.'

'Yes, but –'

Jason frowned. 'My mother used to go on at my gran about her furniture and ornaments and things. "No style," she would say, and my gran would say,

89

"Doesn't matter what you think. You're not living here." M-my mother kept on at her, though, and when Gran died, my m-mother sold the lot to a dealer.'

Rosa subsided, feeling as though she had been put in the wrong somehow, when all she had wanted was to be witty. She bit her tongue when she saw the fishpond and the gnome outside Chrissie's house.

'Bob Morris!' boomed Chrissie's dad as he opened the door. 'And you're Jason Hughes!'

'I know,' said Jason.

'Hahaha! Tell your dad I think he's doing a grand job with the team. Come in! Come in!' He slapped Jason on the back and guided him into the hallway. 'Come in, girls,' he yelled over his shoulder. Meena and Rosa exchanged a look.

'So our Christine's gone and joined a video-making club, has she?' Mr Morris shouted at Jason. 'She gets it from her dad, you know, an interest in films. I run the new multi-screen on the edge of town. Big concern! Huge success!'

Mrs Morris fluttered downstairs, hands poised at shoulder height. Her nails were long and red. Chrissie followed, head down.

'Now, make sure you keep Christine behind the camera, Jason,' giggled Mrs Morris in a girlish voice. 'She's not exactly photogenic. Stand up straight, dear, for goodness sake.'

'No, a bit too much meat on her bones for the camera to love her,' shouted Mr Morris. Rosa stared pointedly at his bulging waistline. 'Not like her sister Barbara. Now there's a beauty!'

Rosa followed his pointing finger to the framed photograph of a girl about three years older than

Chrissie. The family resemblance was there but the eyes were bigger and bluer, the fair hair thick and glossy, the cheek-bones pronounced.

'And you've got two more beauties here, Jason, by the look of it!' roared Mr Morris, slipping his arms around Rosa and Meena. 'Plenty of talent here – for your film, I mean! Hahaha!'

'Well, we're not filming tonight, it's just a planning meeting,' muttered Jason, staring at the carpet.

'Keep an ear out for your little brother, Christine,' warbled Mrs Morris, hands still cocked. 'He's not due a feed until eleven, but there's a bottle ready just in case. I've left some snacks in the kitchen – for your guests, mind, not you! Remember your diet. I hope you're allowed to eat peanuts and things, dear,' she said to Meena, smiling brightly.

'But, I'm not on a diet . . . .' faltered Meena.

'No, dear,' said Mrs Morris, very slowly and clearly. 'I meant your. . . . taboo thingummies, you know. . . . Well, come along, Bob. Byeee!'

'Don't do anything I wouldn't do . . . .'

'Sorry,' groaned Chrissie, pushing the door shut. 'They should have gone half an hour ago.' She shook back her hair and looked around the hallway.

'Where's Mouse?' she said.

Hello, Mum. It's me, Liam. I brought you some flowers, Mum. Yellow ones. Vera at the florists gave them to me for cleaning her front window.

There. They look lovely. Really bright.

They'll last, if the frost doesn't get them. It's a big moon tonight. I can see right down the hill to the town centre. Floodlights on at the City ground. There's a crane still working where they're building the new shopping centre. Did I tell you they're knocking Owens down?

Nice and quiet up here, though. The grave'll need weeding soon. I'll do it next time I come. Vera says she'll give me some daffodil bulbs if I do her window again.

Mum . . . ? Dad's up to his old tricks again. You told me to look after him, but I don't know what to do this time. See, there's this Andrew Greenwood at the school and he's found out. I have to give him stuff to keep him quiet.

Mum. . . . There's these others. They have to give him stuff too. If I go in with them, I'll have to tell them, about Dad and things. But there's a chance they can sort things out and I've no chance at all on my own.

I'm scared, Mum. You know what'll happen this time if. . . . I couldn't stand that. It was bad enough, losing you.

Is it all right, then, if I tell them about Dad? Only, I'm supposed to be there now. I know what you would say. Are they good people? Well, they're clever, Mum. And the teachers like them.

You think I should do it, don't you? For Dad. I'll have to run, then. I should be there now. Goodnight Mum.

God Bless.

7

The Secrets Club

'Well, I'm not surprised, really,' said Chrissie. 'It's probably just as well he hasn't turned up. He is from up that way.'

The other three looked at her.

'Sorry, did I miss something?' said Meena.

'Mouse. He's from up there,' said Chrissie, pointing.

'Mouse lives in your attic?' asked Jason.

'No . . . I mean – '

'You mean – he's an alien from outer space?'

'She means he's from the Hilltop Estate, don't you?' said Rosa, dangerously calm.

'Oh, no! This our worst nightmare!' yelled Jason, in his best sci-fi movie voice. 'In fact, it's worser!'

'Well,' said Chrissie, becoming flustered, 'everyone knows they can't be trusted. My dad won't employ anyone from Hilltop – '

'Oh, great!' Rosa exploded. 'I'm sure those poor blokes traipsing down the hill to the Job Centre every day would be really pleased to hear that!'

'But . . . but . . . I mean, everyone knows that when they want something, they just come down here and steal it from us . . .'

'Welcome to this week's edition of "Them and

Us", coming to you live from Chrissie's hallway,' intoned Jason, in his best BBC voice.

'Why is it that when there's any danger of something getting serious, you try to turn it into a joke?' snapped Rosa.

'And why is it that you blow your top at least once a day and twice on Sundays?' growled Jason, scowling horribly.

The doorbell rang.

'Quick, hide the video!' hissed Jason and Chrissie hung her head.

'Let's start again, shall we?' said Meena.

'Shnerfnudznyargsnyeefnyadze,' said Jason.

'Pardon?'

'I'm re-winding.'

Meena laughed and opened the door for Liam.

There were five squares of folded paper on Chrissie's bedroom carpet. They each picked one and opened it up. Meena sighed and put her square back in the centre. Everyone stared at the number one written there in purple felt tip.

Meena sat very still, concentrating her mind the way she always did in the last few seconds before a race. Then she began. She began with a story that had been smoothed by many tellings, like a pebble rounded by the sea. Her voice took on a lilting rhythm and the words flowed easily.

'When my mother's parents, Naresh and Geeta, left India three months after their wedding, everyone said they were crazy. Their families were respected landowners and traders and, by Indian standards, they were well off. But Naresh and Geeta had grown up during Independence and Partition.

They had lived through all the fighting and bitterness. People they knew had been killed; families destroyed. For a whole summer after Partition, Naresh and Geeta had played by the river in the shadow of a dust cloud which hung above the opposite bank. The dust was kicked up by a crocodile of refugees trekking from state to state, with carts piled high and babies on their backs.

'Naresh and Geeta remembered the babies especially, when the time came to start their own family. They wanted their babies to be safe and healthy and happy. They had heard the stories about Britain. They knew about the hospitals and the schools for everyone. They knew about the jobs that paid more than most people could ever hope to earn in India. So they came here, in the fifties, when the British were still inviting people to fill their factories.

'They found a cold, grey place with "Whites only" signs in the windows of all the flats. They sat in their one room and heard different stories about Britain. They heard about the doctors and teachers from India who were working as hospital porters and school cleaners because their qualifications did not count here. You see, said Naresh and Geeta. We have done the right thing. Our children's qualifications will be recognized wherever they go. Our children will have a British education. They clung to this belief as they stared into the popping gas fire, trying not to think about wide horizons and sun-warmed fruit and freshly caught fish.

'By the time my mother was born, Naresh and Geeta had saved enough from their factory work to start their first shop. By the time she was five, they

95

had two stores and plans for a third. They sent her to school with new shoes and a warm coat and a real leather satchel. They were so proud.

'My mother still has nightmares about her wonderful British education. She has nightmares about what happened to her warm coat and her leather satchel. She has nightmares about the people from the Campaign Against Immigration who stood outside the school, telling children they would catch smallpox if they sat next to her. Most of all, she has nightmares about the immigrant hut. The lights were left on all day in that prefab because of the boards covering the smashed windows. My mother sharpened her pencils into waste paper bins full of broken glass. Sometimes, men came to cover up the words that had been smeared across the outside walls. My mother listened to the rasping strokes of their paintbrushes as she tried to improve her English and learn something called General Knowledge.

'The main thing she learned, though, was to feel unwanted. She left school with nothing. Now, she and my father manage a whole chain of supermarkets and off-licences, but she thinks she is stupid. She thinks it is her fault that she got nothing from a British education.

'So, when I did well at primary school, my family were thrilled. When Mrs Walker said I should go in for an assisted place at Jesmond School, they were overjoyed. A child from their family at a Public School! The very best British education!'

Jason snorted at that and Meena stopped.

'Shut up, will you?' said Rosa. 'We all agreed to just listen, remember? No talking. No judging.'

'Sorry,' Jason whispered. 'Carry on.'

Meena took a deep breath. The others waited silently but, after carrying them so far with her angry fluency, Meena appeared at a loss for words.

' – I – I went in for the exam a-and I . . . . You see, my family had gone out and bought the whole uniform before I even took the tests. Everything on the list. Hockey boots, tennis shoes, regulation track suit . . . They spent a fortune. Do you see? My whole family were waiting for me to prove that Naresh and Geeta were right to come here. You do see?'

Meena looked around the circle and they all nodded their heads in unison. Rosa hooked her fingers deeper into the pile of Chrissie's bedroom carpet and waited for what had to come next.

Meena's head drooped. 'I cheated,' she said, her voice dull. 'I knew I'd be all right on English and General Knowledge. It was the Maths test . . . Calculators weren't allowed but I taped one of those slim-line ones to my leg and I cut a slit in the front of my pleated skirt, where it would be hidden by a fold in the material. I was going to work it all out in my head first, honestly! I – just wanted to check my answers – just check – '

'Oh, that's not really cheating,' began Chrissie, but Meena cut her off.

'Yes! Yes it was! Don't excuse me. I finished the first question. I opened my skirt. I switched on the calculator and then I started to giggle.'

'You – giggled?' asked Rosa.

'It's a nervous thing. I've always had it. My mother says it's my conscience because it only happens when I know I'm doing something wrong. Once it starts, I can't stop.

'We were all lined up at desks in this old hall. It had a high, arched roof and a wooden floor. The noise, my noise, really echoed.' Meena shut her eyes and groaned, biting hard on a knuckle. They screwed up their faces in sympathy, all seeing the girl in the middle of the silent exam hall, laughing and unable to stop.

'The teacher came and led me out – all the way down the long row of faces to the door. They were very nice. Once I'd calmed down, they took the calculator off me, put a line through my first answer and said I could continue. I don't know what I wrote. I failed.

'Only my family and my teacher were told. Everyone else thought I'd just had a fit of hysterics. My family said it was their fault for pushing too hard but I could see they were ashamed of me. They – we – are Hindus and honesty is very important to us. I can't let Andrew tell the whole school now. My family . . . it would . . . And that word, cheat. It would stick for ever. I only slipped up once but I'd always be Meena the cheat, wouldn't I? Every time I got a good mark in an exam, people would think . . .' Meena came to a halt, her voice too thick with tears to carry on.

'It's all right, Meena,' said Rosa. 'Well done. It was hard, being the first. Um, who's next?'

Liam leaned forward and put his square of paper next to Meena's. His hand was shaking.

'Me dad's got a load of nicked CD players in his allotment shed,' said Liam.

Rosa blinked. Just like that? She felt as though

she had settled down to watch a film and only caught the final credits. She glared across at Chrissie, expecting to see a smug expression on her face, but Chrissie had been taken by surprise too. Rosa looked back to Liam. He was sitting on the floor, like the rest of them, but his legs were stuck out rigidly in front of him. His ski jacket was pulled tight around him and he was the only one to have kept his shoes on. God, he feels so out of place, she thought. Forget just listening; he needs some help with this.

'Mouse?' she said. 'How did D-cup find out?'

'His dad heard something down at the bookies.'

'And his dad told him?'

Liam nodded. 'Andrew said a CD player would stop him telling the police, so I took my dad's shed key one night. It was easy. These CD players, they're the sort with headphones. You can carry them in your pocket. It was a stupid thing to do, though. Once he got it he said it was evidence and he'd take it to the police unless I did what I was told. I have to run and get his chips for him, put his bets on, stuff like that.'

'Mouse, why don't you tell your dad?' asked Jason.

'I can't.'

'Would he – hurt you?'

Liam's head shot up. 'My dad would never lay a finger on me! He thinks I don't know about the CD players. He never likes me to know when he's up to his tricks, but I always do.'

There was an awkward silence. Liam's grey eyes grew stormy as he saw what they were thinking and the words began to pour out of him. 'He's not

99

a bad man, my dad. He's not! I know people think we're all a load of outlaws in Hilltop, but we're not! My mum brought us up better than that. It's just, Dad never can turn down a mate, and they know it. He walks into the pub and it's, "Hey, Silver, will you keep this stuff for me, just for a week . . . Hey, Silver, I've got a re-spray job to do on these cars and me regular bloke's let me down . . . Hey, Silver, I've got a load of copper pipes need shifting and your van's just the job. . . ." They know he can't say no to a mate. When Mum was here, she watched him, but now . . . .

'And he never learns. He's always dead surprised when he gets caught. That's why they call him Silver, because he never sees the clouds, just the silver lining. He thinks things'll always work out for the best but they don't. The last time he was caught, the judge told him it'd be prison next. They'll put me in a home if they put my dad in the nick. I can't let that happen – I can't lose him as well. My mum would've done anything to keep the family together . . . Ah, God. I've got to get that CD player back . . .'

'We will, Mouse,' said Jason. 'That's what we're here for.' He ruffled Liam's hair. 'Come in number three, your time is up!' he added, too cheerfully, beaming at Rosa and Chrissie. His jaw muscles were clenched so tightly, it looked more like a snarl.

Rosa leaned forward and dropped her square of paper into the centre. She suddenly envied Meena and Liam the relief of telling their secrets. The urge to do the same grew very strong, but one glance at Jason sent her back to her prepared story.

'The Monday before last, I went into the Old

House after school and I unscrewed one of the stair lions from the bannisters. It took me ages. D-cup came in just as I was putting it into my school bag and he caught me on his nasty little camera. I put the lion back, but he's got a photograph of me stealing school property.'

'You stole one of the stair lions?' spluttered Jason. 'I wish I'd thought of that.'

'No, I tried to steal one,' corrected Rosa.

'Why?' asked Meena.

'Why? Um . . . because I was sick of the place,' Rosa improvised.

'You – sick of school?' asked Chrissie.

'Yes, me! I was suddenly so sick of the place I wanted to bull-doze it into the ground, all right? Only, there weren't any bull-dozers around so I thought it would be, well, a symbolic act to steal one of the lions. They're like Seaton Court mascots, aren't they. We've even got them on our blazer badges.'

'But I thought you loved school?'

'Yeah, yeah. That's what everyone thinks. Red Rosa the loner. Rosa the swot, age fourteen, going on forty. Wouldn't know a joke if it jumped up and bit her on the bum. I know what everyone thinks of me but I didn't mean it to be like this! I mean, I want to do well at school and, yes, I care about stuff like pollution, I really do. But I didn't mean to end up on my own. I didn't want to be avoided like some sort of freak – I don't know how it happened. I – I was just trying to be like my mum and gran, that's all.'

Rose fished out her locket and opened it. 'There they are. They both did so well and they think I'm the same. Rosa's clever, they say. Rosa's independent. Rosa knows exactly what she wants. But I'm not . . . I don't . . . not all the time.'

'That must be a heavy locket to wear,' said Jason, brushing her arm with his fingertips. The touch shattered her defences instantly, like a stone hitting a windscreen. Rosa drew one shocked breath and began to sob. She had told a secret after all; a secret she had not known she was keeping.

'Here,' said Meena, sitting beside her and holding out a tissue. 'We're a right pair, aren't we? Us and our ancestors.'

'My turn,' said Jason, flicking his number over his head. 'I'll keep it short. Good guy keeps private diary of his wild deeds hidden in shed. Bad guy spies on good guy. Bad guy steals diary. Bad guy blackmails good guy.'

Rosa came out from behind her tissue and frowned. 'Why should that bother you? You're always boasting about stuff like that.'

Jason snatched a pink teddy bear from Chrissie's bead and stared into its glassy eyes. 'I care not a whit for myself,' he roared to the bear. 'For my escapades are known throughout the land. Nay, 'tis my friends I must protect, still kept prisoner in those lightless halls from which I have escap'd!'

'He means those schools he got thrown out of,' explained Chrissie to Liam.

'And 'tis for my dear father I fear, him and his band of trusty men! In other words,' said Jason, reverting to his normal voice, 'If the press got hold of some of the stuff in that diary, they'd have a field day. I mean, some of the things we've got up to – me, my dad and the team, that is – '

A piercing wail stopped Jason in mid-boast. He stared at the pink bear. 'How did you do that without moving your lips?' he said.

'It's Josh, silly,' giggled Chrissie, hurrying out of the room.

'And you woke him with all that shouting,' snapped Rosa, glaring at Jason. How could he flip from hearing her cry to performing a double act with a teddy bear? Couldn't he see how hurtful it was? No wonder he had no steady girlfriend; whenever things got serious, he turned into a game show host. She glared even harder but Jason ducked his head and began to rub at a non-existent mark on his knee.

Lying.

He was lying.

Rosa blinked. She looked again at Jason. His ears were red. Suddenly, she was certain he had lied about his secret. There had been something wrong with his confession. Something missing . . . something that always appeared when he was upset . . . Of course! No stutter! Rosa opened her mouth to ask him why he had lied, then she shut it again. Who was she to ask something like that?

Chrissie came back with her baby brother draped over one shoulder and a bottle in her hand. His face was nestled into her neck but, when she turned to shut the door, he lifted his head to stare owlishly at the strangers.

Liam smiled for the first time that evening. He lifted a hand and wiggled his fingers at the baby.

'Hello, Josh. Hello. Oh, he's lovely,' said Meena. 'I can remember when my baby brother looked as sweet as that. He's two years old now and built like a tank! How old is Josh, three months?'

'Seventeen weeks and three days,' smiled Chrissie. She rejoined the circle and sat the baby between her legs, with his back resting against her stomach, then she took the muslin nappy from her shoulder and whisked it around his neck, holding him steady while she tucked in the ends at the back.

'Haircut, sir?' asked Jason.

They all burst out laughing and Josh, who had been regarding them solemnly all this time, jumped at the sudden noise. He looked so comical, with his dark hair sticking up all over his head and his eyes round with surprise, that they laughed again and this time Josh joined in, pumping his arms up and down.

The laughter stopped when Chrissie leaned forward and dropped her square of paper into the centre of the circle. No-one thought it strange that she should place her number on the pile, even though she was the only one left with a secret to tell. They recognized it as a ritual act, a way of beginning, and they settled back to listen.

Chrissie pulled her legs up, crossed them at the ankles, and slotted Josh into the cradle they made. He latched onto the bottle teat and began to suck, his eyes intent on her face. His starfish hands opened and shut, clutching at air until she gave him a finger to grip. His eyes closed and he settled to the feed. Only then did Chrissie look up. The rat-tails of hair that framed her face were quivering and her eyes were hard and bright.

'He's mine,' she said, her expression a strange mixture of pride and fear. 'Josh is my baby.' She

104

bit her lip and waited, looking as though the rest of her life hung on their reactions.

'He's a fine baby,' said Liam. 'Watch him go for that bottle!' He nodded at Josh approvingly then looked at her and smiled. His grey eyes were steady and clear. You and the baby, his look said. Nothing else. Simple.

'Oh, thank you, Mouse,' gasped Chrissie.

'Why didn't you get rid of it?' blurted Jason. 'I mean – not that I think you should've done. I mean, he's great. But most girls would've got rid of it. Not that I think that's wrong either . . . What I mean is things would've been so much easier for you if you'd decided to . . . Ah, forget it, please. I'll shut up now.'

'No, no, it's all right. You see, I didn't really decide anything. I just pretended it wasn't happening. I just – ignored it. I was plump, well, fat anyway, so it didn't show for ages. It just looked like I was putting on more weight. My mum didn't catch on until the end of April, when I kept on wearing baggy jumpers through all that really sunny weather. I was seven months gone by then; too late to have an abortion.'

Rosa was busy calculating. Seven months pregnant in April . . . that means that she must have gone all the way with a boy . . . roughly this time last year. She did it with someone when she was my age! And look what she ended up with. Rosa shuddered. The thought of giving birth made her want to jump up and run away. Her class had seen the dreaded 'having a baby' video only a few weeks before and she had decided that she could never,

ever lie naked and groaning on a table with everyone watching her.

'God, Chrissie, it must've been awful!' said Rosa. 'What did your mum and dad say when they found out?'

Chrissie hung her head. 'They were so angry,' she whispered. 'They . . . said I was a tart with no self-respect and they might have known I'd do something like this because I'd always been no good. They said we had to keep it secret because everybody else would think I was a slag, too. They said no-one would talk to me at school if they knew – '

'Rubbish!' said Jason.

'If you ask me, your mum and dad are the no-good ones,' said Rosa. 'What were they trying to do to you, telling you stuff like that? They should've been supporting you!'

'Well, they didn't throw me out – '

'Big deal!'

'I – I suppose they did what they thought was best for me – '

'Well they were wrong!' snapped Rosa.

'Do you really think so?' asked Chrissie, in a trembling voice.

'They were more than wrong; they were cruel.'

Chrissie let out a great breath of air. Tears brimmed in her eyes and began to roll down her cheeks in a steady trickle. She put down the empty bottle and eased the sleeping baby on to her shoulder. 'It's been horrible,' she said, patting Josh's back. 'They took me out of school. Told everyone I had glandular fever and said I was too ill for visitors. When the baby started coming, my mum left me at the hospital and told them to 'phone her when it was all over. They put me in a side ward on my own. They kept calling me Mrs.'

'Where the hell was the father?' asked Rosa.

'He doesn't know. He wouldn't be interested anyway. He was my first – my only – boyfriend, so you see they were wrong about me being a slag. I wasn't sleeping around, or anything.'

'But you had sex with this boy,' Meena pointed out, speaking for the first time. Rosa glanced at her sharply, but Chrissie was too wrapped up in what she was saying to catch the note of disapproval.

'Yes. I didn't want to but I did it anyway. He kept saying that if I loved him, I would.'

'Look, Chrissie, you don't have to tell us any more . . . don't say any more,' said Jason, turning away from her tear-streaked face, but Chrissie kept on talking. After a year of silence, there was a lot of misery to come out. Jason jumped up and hurried to the window, staring out into the darkness while she told the rest of her story.

'The joke was, I didn't love him. Not really. I didn't want to do it but I just couldn't say no. Isn't that pathetic? I wanted someone to like me, that's all. My mum and dad were right about me having no self-respect. You've got to have a bit of belief in yourself to say no to people. We did it three times and I hated every minute of it. Then he finished with me.'

'I'd like to kill him!' fumed Rosa. 'Hadn't he heard about Aids? Where did he think babies came from, the stork fairy? Why didn't you make him use a condom?'

'I – I thought he was. At least, he said he would

107

take care of it, so I just shut my eyes and let him get on with it.'

Josh began to whimper into Chrissie's neck.

'Come on, big man,' said Liam. 'Let's take a walk and see if we can't shake out that wind.' He took Josh from Chrissie and strolled around the room, making a steady, gentle shushing noise. Chrissie watched until she was sure he knew what he was doing, then she continued.

'Right up until he was born, my mum and dad wanted me to have the baby adopted. He was due at the end of June, you see. They said I'd have the summer holidays to get over it before I went back to school, all better after my glandular fever. But when it turned out to be a boy and they saw how beautiful he was, they changed their minds.

'So, we all moved up here. They were moving anyway, because of my dad's work, but the plan had been for me to stay with my aunt this year to finish my exam courses at my old school.

'At first, my mum said to let people think Josh was my little brother just until I'd got the feel of the place and made some friends. After a few weeks, she said it was best not to say anything that would give me a bad reputation while I was still at school. Now she's saying it would be bad for Josh later if people knew he was illegitimate and why don't I leave him with them when I go to college?'

'Don't you think that's a generous offer?' asked Meena.

'No. I know them. They're after Josh. They've always wanted a son. They were really disappointed when I came along instead. She's even started pretending in the house. When I come in from school, she says to him, "Here's your big sister". I take him into bed with me now, when he wakes up at night, and I hold him while he goes back to sleep, and I whisper, "I'm your mum, Josh. I'm your mum" . . .'

'Why on earth didn't you just tell them where to get off?' asked Rosa.

'Because when Andrew came after me for free cinema passes, I thought they must be right, about people seeing me as a slut. He was saying exactly what they'd predicted! And . . . and right now I just haven't got the energy for a fight – not on top of school and the baby and D-cup . . . I'm surviving, that's all.'

'They're back,' said Jason, turning from the window.

The front door slammed. Feet thudded up the stairs.

'Coo-ee! You forgot your snack tray,' called Mrs Morris, bursting into the room without knocking. She caught sight of Liam holding Josh, and her smile slipped.

'Um . . . this is Liam, mum,' said Chrissie. 'He's part of our club.'

'I see,' said Mrs Morris, taking in the greasy ski jacket Josh was snuggling against and the nicotine-stained fingers supporting his head. Liam looked down at the carpet. He wished he'd had time to clean his fingernails after weeding his mum's grave. He wanted to shove his hands deep into his pockets, but how could he when he was holding Josh? He was relieved when Mrs Morris put down the tray with a clatter and plucked the baby from his arms.

'Keeping your brother up – you should know better, Christine Jane Morris.'

'Mum, he woke up! I'll put him back in his cot – '

'No, leave him to me. I think you've done enough for one night.'

Chrissie stood up and tried to take Josh.

'Christine!' said Mrs Morris, snatching him away. Josh began to cry.

'See? Now little Robert's upset,' said Mrs Morris, whisking Josh out of the room.

'Robert?' said Meena, as soon as the door closed.

'She's started calling him that, after my dad,' sighed Chrissie, grabbing a handful of peanuts and stuffing them into her mouth.

'Listen, Chrissie,' said Rosa, fiercely. 'You don't have to put up with this. I'm sure there are ways of keeping Josh and going to college. There are creches and . . . and, you know, all sorts. We're going to find out about it, all right? But first, we're going to sort out D-cup, because it's five against one now. The next one he calls in for a little bullying session is going to have Jason's mini-cassette in their pocket and a film crew backing them up. D-cup hasn't got a chance against The Secrets Club!'

'All right!' said Jason, punching the air. 'The Secrets Club!'

'The Secrets Club!' echoed Chrissie and Meena. Liam took his hands out of his pockets and grinned.

Hello, Josh. And what sort of time is this to wake your mum, hmmm? Oh, smiling, is it? Smiling now, is it? Come on, let's sit by the window and wrap ourselves in this nice big quilt and you can have your bottle. That's it.

I've got ten pence for you, from Mouse. He says in his family it's traditional to give a new baby luck money. It's our first present, Josh. Fancy Mouse being the one to give it to us. You know, he can't be all bad, if he likes babies. Oh, but the look on your gran's face when she saw him ...

She loved the others, though. Well, they're everything I'm not, aren't they? Brainy ... beautiful ... rich ... That's why it's got to be one of them with the cassette recorder, not me, Josh. Not me. It's so important to get it right, you see, and I know I'd get it wrong.

That's why I didn't say anything about me taking those tickets to D-cup after half-term. I opened my mouth to tell them, honestly, then I thought, no I'll only make a right dog's dinner of it. Let's face it, I get an E minus for most things – except you, of course. And my stories. I like my stories. You can read them when you're older. Maybe I'll be a famous writer by then, and we'll buy an island, somewhere hot ...

... Josh – what if ... what if when I went to see D-cup, I pretended I was writing one of my stories? I bet I could get him to talk about blackmail on the tape, if I pretended I was sorting out a page of dialogue – I wouldn't be nearly so scared!

Oh, dear. I can't decide. If I did it, they'd stop thinking I was such a wimp, especially Rosa, but if I made a mess of it, we'd all be finished. What shall I do, Josh?

8

Windows

The cam-corder buzzed on the window-sill like a huge bluebottle as Meena zoomed in on the green painted door in the Old House back yard. She looked through the eye-piece and then wedged one more text book between the cam-corder and the sill.

'There,' said Meena. 'The angle's right and it's steady enough. We should get it all in shot, but the yard's pretty much in shadow. I'm not sure whether there's enough light.' She looked up at the grey November sky, then down at Rosa. 'Give me your jacket a minute.'

Rosa held up the jacket and Meena draped it over the cam-corder so that only the lense was peeping out. 'There. If he does look up, he'll just see a coat and a pile of books. I can't quite believe we're finally going to get him, can you?' she asked, settling down on the English classroom floor next to Rosa. 'First day back at school, as well; I wasn't expecting it to happen so quickly! Chrissie did say lunch-time, didn't she?'

Rosa glanced at her watch. 'Plenty of time, yet,' she said. 'I hope Chrissie doesn't lose her nerve; she looked a bit green when I slipped her the cassette recorder at the lockers this morning. Still, she sounded determined on the 'phone last night. In fact she didn't sound like Chrissie at all – none of the usual umming and ahhing. I think I misjudged – '

'Shhh! I thought I heard something in the corridor,' hissed Meena.

Rosa listened. 'I can't hear anything. Anyway, Mouse is out there, guarding that fire door like a little pit bull terrier. He won't let anything come down that corridor without warning us first. Unless – '

'What?' whispered Meena, her eyes wide.

' – Unless it's the ghost of the Old House upstairs maid come to haunt us!'

Meena grinned. 'Oh, no. We'll be dusted to death!'

'Or she'll just keep pouring tea for us until we burst.'

They leaned together, giggling and shushing.

'Arrgh! Battered to death with a Chelsea bun,' spluttered Rosa. Meena stuffed her school tie into her mouth and collapsed against the radiator.

'Oh, no. Come on,' moaned Rosa. 'We've got to be serious here. Any sign of Chrissie yet?'

Meena peered over the window sill and shook her head.

'Mouse was wearing those old school clothes of your brother's. Did you notice?' asked Rosa.

Meena gave a pleased smile. 'I'm glad. He might as well get some wear out of them; they're too small for Sandeep now.'

'It was a nice thing to do. Mind you, I thought Jason went a bit over the top the next day, bringing

113

that bag full of designer shirts. One of them was silk!'

'Guess what,' began Meena, her eyes dancing. ' – Oh no, I can't tell you!'

'Meena! What?'

'All right, if you promise not to tell Jason. I saw Mouse's sister wearing the silk one in town on Friday, and remember that other shirt, the purple one with all the swirly bits? Her friend was wearing that!'

'No!' Rosa peered out of the window then settled back against the radiator. 'It was a good half-term, wasn't it?'

'Yes. We were all very . . . gentle with one another.'

Rosa blinked at Meena's description, then nodded. Gentle was exactly the right word.

'Talking about gentle, we met Mouse's dad last night, me and Jason. He was really nice.'

'How did that happen?'

'It was Jason's idea. He said we'd have to go and tell Mouse because he's not on the 'phone, so we biked over there. It took us ages to find it.' Rosa stopped, remembering the journey through the dark maze of pot-holed roads, smashed street-lights and missing street names.

'The road where they live, it's . . .' she hesitated, not sure how to describe the bleak, treeless length of Tipton Avenue. It had been a struggle to force their bikes up the long rise to Liam's house against a constant wind which blasted down from the top of the hill and whistled through the windows of abandoned council houses. Once, a pack of stray dogs had stopped worrying at a pile of rubbish sacks and trotted into the road in front of them. One big mongrel with yellow eyes and a tail curled over its back like a question mark had even nipped at her tyres.

'And his house, Meena. It was like a – a war zone. The front gate and part of the wall had been knocked down. I think it was so somebody could get these two cars into the garden. They were just stuck up on bricks in all the long grass and there were bits of engine and stuff all over the place. A couple of windows were boarded up and some kids'd been having a party with spray cans on the side wall of the house.' Rosa shook her head.

'I thought Mouse was going to be so embarrassed when we knocked at the door, but he was really pleased to see us. I didn't know what to say, but Jason was great. He handed out these bags of chips he'd bought down the road and said he'd love a cup of tea and he sprawled in front of the fire as if he was at home. It was quite cosy, really, as long as you didn't look at the black mould under the window or the damp patch on the ceiling.'

'You don't seem to mind him as much as you used to,' said Meena. 'Jason, I mean. I'll never forget that look you gave me when I brought him to that first meeting.'

'Well, he's not quite the selfish little show-off I thought he was,' said Rosa. 'In fact, he's been almost OK this past week.' If you forget that he's lying about his secret, she added, silently. 'But don't you dare tell Natalie Cooke I said that.'

'Why on earth would I want to talk to Natalie Cooke?' said Meena, kneeling up at the window.

'She's about as exciting as wallpaper paste. Oops! Action stations! Here comes Chrissie.'

Chrissie stopped at the edge of the yard and stared across at the green painted door. Jason was just around the corner, ready to jump in if she called for him, but still she was terrified. She knew the cassette recorder was invisible from every angle because she had stood in front of the toilet mirror for ten minutes, but she felt as though huge, neon arrows were pointing to her blazer pocket.

I can't do this. Oh, why did I think I could do this? Because it's a story, remember? And you're good at stories. OK. Now walk over to the door . . . and knock. Go on, knock!

Footsteps clumped up the concrete staircase. The door opened and Chrissie shook back her hair. Then Andrew surged out, clamped his hands on to her shoulders and ran her into the wall. Instinctively, her arms shot up to protect her face and her elbows and chest took the worst of the impact. A burning pain shot from her elbows to her finger-tips and the breath was knocked out of her. She was struggling to fill her lungs again when he twisted her round to face him and smacked the heel of his hand up under her chin. Her head snapped back, hitting the brickwork with a crack.

'Thought you could fool me, did you?' he grated.

Chrissie tried to shake her head, but his hand was gripping her jaw, forcing her head back against the wall. His palm pressed against her lips, hot and rubbery, and she could smell fish and chips on his fingers. Her stomach heaved. How could he know their plan? She tried to lever her head free to shout

116

for Jason but he just leaned on her face until she stopped.

'Don't pretend you don't know what I'm talking about, slag. I saw you behind the music block.'

For a second, Chrissie froze. What did he mean? Then she remembered the first Secrets Club meeting two weeks ago, under the willow tree. Of course! He had seen them there! She slumped with relief.

'Yes, you know what I'm talking about, don't you, slag? Surprised? But I told you, I know everything that goes on in this school. I've already put Rosa Morgan right. Now I want to hear your story.' He released her jaw and Chrissie took a few gulps of air while she tried to remember the cover story they had worked out.

'I – I'm sorry, Andrew – '

'Mr Greenwood to you, slag.'

' – Mr Greenwood. She just asked me to meet her there. She didn't say why. As soon as I knew what she was trying to do, I said no. I didn't want any trouble . . .'

'Yeah, well just make sure you keep it like that.' Andrew leaned against the door frame and held out his hand, suddenly bored.

Make him say it, thought Chrissie, trying to look bewildered.

'Give me the tickets,' sighed Andrew.

'Wh-which tickets?'

'The cinema tickets, you brainless slag!'

Well done, thought Chrissie, fumbling in her bag. Now, the blackmail. Get him on to the blackmail.

'Um, Mr Greenwood? H-how long . . . how long is this going to go on?'

Andrew's bored expression faded and a slow grin

117

spread across his face. 'Oh, she wants dates, now. Well let me see, I'll have to look in my appointments diary.' He flicked the pages of an imaginary book. 'Hmm . . . Monday, haircut. Tuesday, dentist. Wednesday, blackmail that slag Christine Morris until I get tired of seeing her ugly face because tarts like her deserve nothing better! How long?' he roared, grabbing the hair above her ear and twisting it upwards until she felt her scalp would rip. 'How long?'

'Owww! Don't . . . I'm sorry . . .'

'You are a diseased slag. Say it!'

'I am a diseased slag.'

'Again.'

'Owww! I am a diseased slag!'

'Your baby should have died at birth. Say it!'

'No – Please –'

'Say it.'

'Oh, Josh –'

'Say it!' shouted Andrew, twisting his fist more tightly into her hair.

Chrissie rose up on her toes, trying to ease the pain. Andrew yanked his fist higher.

'My – baby – should have – died – at birth.'

Andrew walked out of the yard and Meena reached up to switch off the cam-corder. Tears stood in her eyes. Rosa got up from her knees and gripped the sill to stop her hands from shaking. She had been hugely shocked when D-cup burst into the yard. A week away from him had blurred her memories but one glimpse of his looming bulk brought everything back into sharp focus. It was the mix of size and menace that was so frightening; even the way he

118

stared and stood too close was a kind of violence. Her mind kept re-running the scene where he had grabbed Chrissie by the shoulders and slammed her into the wall. There had been no hesitation there; no holding back. He hadn't even stopped to check the windows for watchers first. He's beginning to think he can get away with anything, she thought, and shuddered. Had she really imagined they could stop him with the Secrets Club? Rosa thought of the photograph she had seen on the front page of the newspapers she delivered that morning. It was of a group of children clutching plywood swords and standing in the path of a tank.

'Never-Never Land,' she said, and her voice shook. 'That's where we've been.'

Meena nodded. They did not look at one another.

Jason hurried into the yard below and helped Chrissie to her feet. His face was grim as he looked up at their window.

'I watched him as far as the bungalow,' he called up softly. 'Move to the room across the corridor, OK? Then we'll have a view down to the gates in case he heads back up here. We're coming up.'

Chrissie touched her fingers to the side of her head and winced. The skin around her ear and hairline was red and swollen.

'Are you all right?' asked Meena. 'That looks like it's going to bruise.'

'It was worth it,' said Chrissie, 'Because I did it! Me! I got it all on tape.' She handed the cassette recorder to Jason, smiling proudly.

'You were brilliant,' said Rosa, turning from the window. 'And he was an utter – '

'I don't believe it,' Jason interrupted softly. He threw the cassette recorder down on the table. 'The tape's still at the start. We haven't got anything.'

'What? Let me see that.' Meena picked up the machine.

'Oh, no,' Chrissie moaned. 'I knew I shouldn't've done it. I can never do anything right. I should've left it to – '

'No, it's not your fault,' said Meena, pressing buttons. 'This is broken. There's nothing working. It must have happened when he pushed you against that wall.'

Chrissie began to cry. Jason rested his forehead on the formica table top and covered his head with his arms. 'Hang on,' said Meena. 'There's still the cam-corder. Do you want to look at it, Rosa? I've re-wound it.'

Rosa shook her head and turned back to staring out of the window. There was a dreadful chill in the pit of her stomach. Meena shrugged and hefted the cam-corder on to her shoulder. The machine hummed for several minutes but Meena said nothing and her silence told them more than any words.

'It was too dark, wasn't it,' said Rosa, when Meena gently replaced the camcorder in its case.

'Just a lot of shadows,' sighed Meena. 'It could be anything. You can't even tell they're people some of the time.'

Chrissie's weeping reached a new level and Rosa jumped down from the window-sill to comfort her. Meena took her place on watch and Jason picked up his cassette recorder.

'You know, there's always the next time,' he said.

'If I could get this fixed . . .' He bent his head to the machine and no-one noticed when Liam slipped from the room.

He jumped down the steps at the front of the Old House and began jogging down the hill, swearing steadily. His rucksack flapped against his back, beating out a rhythm to match the swearing and the jogging. Liam fell into the rhythm and was lulled by it and failed to notice the mutants huddled under a tree outside the school gates, sharing a cigarette. They had time to unfurl and spread across his path before he looked up and saw them.

Liam skidded to a halt and stood, feeling his heart punch against his ribs.

'Oh, dear,' said School-tie, making a great show of looking at his watch. 'You won't get down to the shop and back in time for the bell, you know. What's the matter, run out of fags, have you?'

'No,' said Liam, then he bit his tongue.

'So,' grinned School-tie, 'You have got some on you. And we're all out of them, aren't we, lads?'

The others nodded, closing in. Liam sighed and fished the cigarette pack from his pocket.

'Aha,' said School-tie, cupping a hand to his ear. 'Did I hear money jingling?'

'No. I've no money,' said Liam, backing off.

'No? I think we'll just have a little look in your pockets, shall we?'

Liam flicked open the pack, threw the cigarettes into the air and raced back into school. Once through the gates, he turned sharp right and ran straight at the high fence around the caretaker's bungalow. He jumped, reaching up with both hands, and just managed to hook his fingers over the top of the fence. By the time they had picked up the cigarettes and followed him through the gates, Liam was wrapped around the trunk of a large rhododendron bush in the bungalow garden.

The mutants soon gave up the search and straggled back to the shelter of their tree. Liam relaxed, and settled down to wait for the bell, when it would be safe to come out again. He lifted his head and stared straight at Andrew Greenwood.

For the second time in a few minutes, Liam's heart knocked against his ribs. Andrew was standing a few metres away, profiled in one of the bungalow windows. Slowly, Liam eased round the bush until there was a screen of glossy green leaves between him and the bungalow, then he became very still, watching.

The light was on in the room. Liam could see posters on the walls and a single bed with a large tin box resting on it. The box was open and Andrew was going through the contents, lifting them out one by one. Some papers, a leather-bound book, a small CD player . . . .

Liam felt a thrill run down his spine as he realized what he was seeing. All their secrets were there in that battered tin box! Andrew threw in Chrissie's cinema tickets, closed the lid and clicked the padlock shut. Then he slid the box under his bed.

Out in the garden, Liam hugged himself. 'Easy,' he breathed, studying the catch on the bedroom window. He waited until Andrew had settled down on the bed, then he backed towards the fence, always keeping the lit window in sight.

At last, his hands touched the rough wooden slats of the fence. Liam threw one last glance towards the window, then he took a deep breath, turned and swarmed up the fence like a gekko. As Liam flipped over the top, Andrew frowned on the bed, his eye caught by a flash of red, white and blue in his bedroom mirror. He rolled off the bed and stared from his window at the empty garden. His eyes narrowed and he turned for the door.

For a few seconds Liam crouched on the other side of the fence, picking splinters from his hands. He had a choice to make. Did he go back to the others, or did he do this on his own? Liam hesitated then stood up and headed for the gates. A few steps later he remembered the mutants and stopped. Then he shrugged his shoulders, turned, and jogged back up to the Old House.

Peering through a knot-hole in the fence, Andrew watched Liam all the way up the hill. His big hands clenched once, then reached out and tore a small branch from a nearby bush, snapping it into tiny pieces.

Date: Monday, 3rd November.
Time: Don't know. Late. Dark.
Place: The mattress, my shed.

Dire Dearie,

I said I'd never do this again. Write a diary, that is. Not after what happened to the last one. But, here I am. Maybe that shrink was right about me having an addictive person-ality.

It's all set for Wednesday. D-cup'll be out at the mid-week match (with *my* tickets) and it's dog track and bingo night for the parents. Mouse says he can open the window. We just go in, get the box, and our worries are over.

They're scared – and they're expecting me to be Mr Cool. They think burglary's a doddle for someone who's been expelled three times. They were going on about my swimming pool trick and the thing with the acid on the cricket pitch and Rosa Morgan was looking at me as though I was a complete prat. I could see it in her beautiful eyes. I think she likes me a bit more than she did, though. Or hates me a bit less.

Maybe, when this is all over... We'd be good together. Dark and fair. No, she'd run a mile. The trouble is, she doesn't like jokes and I can't match her brain power. I always seem to say the wrong thing and then she gives me that look. God, she has got beautiful eyes...

About Wednesday. The truth is, anyone can do stuff like the swimming pool trick when they don't care about getting caught. But this is important. This has got to work, for all of us.

The truth is, I'm as scared as the rest of them.

9

Fireworks

The crack of the explosion was so loud, Meena felt as though she had been punched in the head. She jumped, then jumped again as a second blast rang out.

'Oh, where is he?' she said, flinching as a rocket screamed overhead. 'You don't think he's waiting at the main gates?'

Rosa peered round the corner of the bungalow fence. 'I can't see anything,' she whispered, crouching down again beside the dustbin. 'Anyway, he was the one who said to meet behind here, so we wouldn't be seen.'

'Um, maybe we should, you know, leave it?' quavered Chrissie, staring at the Private sign on the bungalow gate. 'I mean – ' she pointed a shaking finger at the sky, which was fizzing with the sparkling fall-out of exploding rockets.

'No,' hissed Rosa. 'Guy Fawke's Night's the best time! No-one'll notice us, with all this going on.'

'It's definitely empty,' said Jason, his face pressed to the gap between the garden gate and the fence. 'I've been watching for ages – the whole bungalow's dark. Let's go in.'

'Wait. I'll go to the gate and have one more look for Mouse, first.'

Rosa scurried across the grass and flattened herself against the gate post as a car turned in at the school, gravel crunching under its wheels. She stared after the red tail lights, following them up the hill. The whole place was busy. C block and the tall, ground floor windows of the Old House were lit up for evening classes and the car park for the new sports centre was full. Rosa felt a spiky excitement run through her at the thought of all those people up there learning French or swimming through the bright waters of the pool or throwing pots while below them, the Secrets Club were about to commit a robbery.

Except we're not really stealing, thought Rosa, gazing up into the dark bowl of the sky. And as for breaking-in, she added, watching a rocket explode over the Old House, well – this is war. We're striking a blow for freedom!

She slid round the gate post and peered along the road. Already a smoky haze shrouded the streetlights and the air was spiced with the tang of cordite. There was no sign of Liam. 'OK. So we go over the top without reinforcements,' she muttered and hurried back to the others.

'I don't believe it!' whispered Jason, staring at Andrew's window. 'It's open!'

'What?' Rosa squinted through the leaves of the rhododendron bush. 'Oh, you're right! It's just a little gap, but I bet I could get my arm through there and lift the catch.'

'Are – are you sure it's the right window?' asked Chrissie without much hope.

'Yes. Directly opposite the bush, just like Mouse said.'

'I – I still think we should wait for Mouse, even if the window is open. We did agree that we all had to be here, to share the blame if there was any trouble.'

'Look, Chrissie. Let's just get it over with,' sighed Meena. 'And remember, whatever happens, we meet up at Jason's shed.'

Rosa slid her arm through the window and lifted the catch. The window swung open silently, as she knew it would. She was full of a certainty that nothing could go wrong.

'I'm the smallest. I'll go in and hand out the box,' she said, with such confidence that nobody argued.

Jason and Chrissie lifted her to the sill and she eased down into the room. Her eyes adjusted quickly to the deeper darkness and she felt sure-footed and dangerous as she glided across the floor.

She reached the bed and thrust her hand underneath it, expecting to touch cold metal. There was nothing. She swung her arm in a wider arc. Still nothing. She shuffled along on her knees, sweeping her arm back and forth under the bed.

There was no box.

Rosa began to sweat. She stood up and began to work her way around the room, patting at anything that looked like a box.

'What's the matter?' whispered Jason from the window.

'The box – it's not under the bed,' she hissed.

'Are you sure? Let me look.' Jason scrambled into the room, followed by Meena.

'Don't leave me out here!' squeaked Chrissie, hauling herself over the sill and thudding to the floor.

'No, nothing,' muttered Jason, emerging from under the bed. 'Close the curtains. We'll have to risk a light.'

They all saw the sheet of paper taped to the mirror as soon as Meena flicked on the lamp. There were three words scrawled on it in red felt tip.

THE SUCKERS' CLUB

'Oh, no. He's on to us. He's on to the Secrets Club,' moaned Chrissie.

'So that's why the window was open,' breathed Jason. 'He knew we were coming.'

'And I know who told him,' said Chrissie. 'That Liam!'

'Mouse wouldn't do that!' protested Rosa.

'Where is he then? It was that Liam O'Donnell, I'm telling you. Oh, come on. Let's go,' said Chrissie, heading for the window.

'Not yet,' said Rosa, glaring at the message. 'That's just what D-cup thinks we'll do. But first, we're going to check the rest of the house. Our stuff's got to be here somewhere.'

'Are you mad – ?' began Meena. Rosa turned on her, eyes blazing.

'Yes, I'm mad! I am so mad! Come on! He's got us anyway – what's five more minutes? If we could just find that box . . .'

Meena was shaking her head. 'No. To go through their house. It's wrong.'

'You go home, if you like,' said Rosa. 'I'm doing it.'

'I'll wait,' said Meena, quietly. 'But I won't look through their things.'

'All right then. Suit yourself. Chrissie, you check his wardrobe. Jason, you – '

'I'm coming with you,' interrupted Jason.

Rosa padded down the hallway, checking rooms all the way. She had to force herself to open doors, imagining D-cup behind each one, statue-still in the darkness, with rocket flares glittering in his eyes. She would open the door and he would swing round in the chair, his skull earring dancing and his mouth stretching in a grin . . .

At last, there was only one room left, next to the front door. Rosa waited until Jason was right behind her, then she put out her hand and pushed the door open. It was the main sitting room. The hall light touched on two high-backed wing chairs, arranged in front of the fire, but left their depths in shadow. Holding her breath, Rosa reached for the light switch. The chairs were empty. Behind her, Jason sighed with relief.

'So, he really did go to the match,' he said, echoing her thoughts.

'Yes. He doesn't think much of us, does he?'

'No. Still, perhaps it's made him careless. Perhaps our stuff is here somewhere,' said Jason. 'OK. Let's start – '

The scrape of a key slotting into a lock stopped him short. They stared, horrified, as the front door opened.

'Andrew? You're back early – '

A woman stepped into the hallway and stopped

short, blinking at them in the bright light. She was small and bird-thin, but with a sort of scrawny toughness about her. Rosa had seen her around the school, wearing a pink overall and operating a huge floor polishing machine, but she had never connected this dark, wiry person with Andrew.

'Oh,' said the woman and Rosa tensed, watching her mouth, waiting for the scream. Instead, the mouth broke into a smile. 'Oh, really,' she said, whipping off her headscarf and patting her thick, greying hair. 'He should've told me he was bringing you home. I haven't got anything in. No, I tell a lie – I've got some nice Battenburg in the tin. Andrew called it window cake, when he was little. Can I have some window cake, Mum, he used to say. You're Jason, aren't you?' she said, taking off her coat and bustling over to a glass fronted sideboard.

'And you must be Chrissie.' She smiled at Rosa and Rosa tried to smile back, but her cheek muscles quivered so much, she had to give up.

'We'll use the best china, shall we?' said Mrs Greenwood, gently lifting a squat, over-gilded teapot from the sideboard and blowing the dust off it. 'You know, I've been on at him for ages to bring you home and he goes and does it when I'm out! It's a good job I came back early, or I'd have missed you. I didn't fancy staying out late tonight, not with all those bangers going off.'

Mrs Greenwood bent her head and began dusting out the ugly cups with a napkin, treating each one as though it was a piece of Dresden. Rosa sent Jason a desperate look.

130

'Um – actually Mrs Greenwood, we were just going – '

'Nonsense! You'll stay for some tea. It's the least I can do. You've both been so nice to Andrew,' she added, lowering her voice. 'Taking him to the pictures and the football and all that. He's been a lot happier since he made some friends.'

'Oh. Good,' said Rosa, backing towards the door.

'Where is he, anyway? Andrew! Come out here and give me a hand, will you?'

'He – just had to pop out for a minute. We'll go and look for him,' said Jason, reaching for the door knob.

'Yes, we won't be long,' said Rosa, stepping on his heels, and praying that Meena and Chrissie had enough sense to get out through the window.

That was when the wailing started. It was a dreadful noise, full of pain and sadness, rising eerily through the higher octaves in a series of halting jumps. It was coming from Andrew's bedroom.

Mrs Greenwood gave a low scream and her hands clenched, snapping the handle from the cup she was holding. She ran to join Rosa and Jason, and they all stared down the hallway at the door of Andrew's room.

'Is it a cat?' asked Mrs Greenwood, listening to the tormented howls.

'Oh no, what about Chrissie and Meena – ' began Rosa.

'Of course!' Jason cut in. 'It's her conscience!' He hurried down the hallway to Andrew's room and emerged seconds later with his arm around Meena. The noises were coming out of her mouth. She saw Mrs Greenwood and pressed a hand to her lips, but the noises kept coming. Her dark eyes stared out over her fingers, shining with tears.

'The door!' called Jason. Rosa swung it open and he hurried Meena outside. Chrissie followed, head down.

The three of them disappeared behind the bungalow fence and the wailing faded. 'She – she gets a nervous giggle,' said Rosa, and her voice sounded loud in the quiet hallway.

'You call that a giggle?' said Mrs Greenwood, staring out of the open front door. She shuddered, then turned to look at Rosa. Her eyes were bleak.

'Are there any more of you?'

Rosa shook her head.

'You're not his friends,' said Mrs Greenwood, flatly.

Rosa shook her head again and bit her lip. 'We didn't take anything, honestly. We haven't touched a thing. We were just – looking for something . . .'

'What's he done now?'

'He . . .' Rosa looked at the little woman standing in front of her, holding her broken cup. She's his mother, she thought, and her throat closed up. Mrs Greenwood continued to stare at her for a moment, her face full of an angry sorrow. Then her shoulders slumped and she bowed her head.

'That bad, is it?' she sighed, automatically trying to fit the cup and its handle back together.

' – I – can I go now?'

'Yes. You'd better.'

Rosa stepped out of the door, then turned to close it behind her.

'You don't need to tell Andrew that you saw

me,' said Mrs Greenwood, still looking down at the broken cup in her hands.

'No. I'm – really sorry,' said Rosa, easing the door shut. As she ran down the path to join the others, she thought she heard the faint crash of breaking crockery.

Liam was waiting for them on the steps of the summerhouse.

'See!' shrilled Chrissie, pointing an accusing finger. Suddenly, she didn't look like Chrissie at all. Her mild, pale face had been replaced by an unyielding mask and the expression on the mask was an old one, passed down through centuries of religious burnings and racist beatings. Chrissie was on the hunt for a scapegoat to take the blame.

Jason glanced at her uneasily. 'Listen, Chrissie. Just let him speak first,' he muttered, fishing the key from his pocket and hurrying down the garden to open the door.

They filed into the shed. No-one sat down. Liam huddled into his ski-jacket, with his head low. The staccato rattle of fireworks sounded loudly through the thin wooden walls, emphasizing the silence inside.

'Mouse?' said Rosa.

'I've got a message from D-cup,' said Liam. 'He says he hopes we enjoy the next few days, because we're all in for a shock, starting from Monday.'

'That's it, then,' said Meena, softly. 'We've had it.'

'Christ!' said Jason, kicking at a bean-bag.

'You told him, didn't you?' snapped Chrissie. 'You little traitor!'

'I had to!' said Liam. 'He'd seen me, in his garden. He said if I didn't tell him everything, he was going to take that CD player down the nick – '

'So, why didn't you make up a story? Anything?'

'I was scared – he was hurting me!' Liam finally raised his head to look at Chrissie. A rocket flared overhead and they all saw the bruising around his eye, livid in the flickering orange light.

'Oh, Mouse,' sighed Meena.

'That's the first time he's hurt someone where it shows,' muttered Jason. 'You were right, Rosa. He's beginning to think he can do anything.'

Chrissie turned away from his black eye, her face sullen. 'After all we did for you, giving you clothes and that,' she muttered, unwilling to abandon her witch-hunt. 'You Hilltop lot, you can't be trusted.'

'Ah, shut up, Chrissie,' snapped Rosa. 'Your dad's prejudices are showing again. I mean, look around you. Nobody else is blaming Mouse, are they?'

'Well . . .' Jason hesitated. 'I don't think I could do it, betray my mates.'

'Oh, my,' said Rosa, rounding on him. 'How very noble. I suppose you made them all swear that, did you, at your posh private school, before you trotted off on your Boy's Own Adventures? Did they have to stand up and shout, "death before betrayal" and sign their names in blood to get in on your spiffing little wheezes? Well, welcome to the real world, Jason Hughes, where dads get put in prison and boys get put in homes. Don't you dare criticize Mouse until you've had to live like him, all right?'

Jason clenched his fists and took a step towards

134

Rosa, eyes blazing. It seemed a long time before he finally spoke.

'You know your trouble? You look at someone and you think of a Label. That's how you see people, isn't it? In neat little compartments with fancy Labels on them. Meena's right-on, because she's from a Minority Group. Mouse can't do any wrong because he's from the Poor Oppressed Working Class. On the other hand, Chrissie's a bit dodgy because she's got gnomes in her garden and her parents probably vote Conservative. Mind you, she went up in your estimation a bit when you found out she was a Single Parent. Me, I'm the bottom of the pile. Rich Capitalist Fascist Sexist Parasites can't possibly be any good.'

'I don't – '

'Shut up! I haven't finished yet. You think you're so caring, but you don't really understand people at all. You're a snob, Rosa. A cold, intolerant snob. I saw the look on your face when we walked through Chrissie's estate . . . And when we went to Mouse's house – I'm surprised they didn't throw you out, the way you were sitting on that chair as if you might catch something!'

Rosa sensed Liam looking at her, but she couldn't raise her head. She was remembering how she had perched on the edge of her seat, not wanting her hair to touch the chair back. Had it been so obvious? She swallowed down her shock, glad of the semi-darkness of the shed.

Jason glared at her for a few seconds more, waiting for her to snap right back at him, but Rosa was silent. 'Anyway,' he continued, more softly, 'I think Chrissie has got a right to be angry. Mouse didn't think of us at all, only his dad. He could've at least told us D-cup knew about the break-in.'

'No, we have no right to be angry,' said Meena, calmly. 'We don't own Mouse just because we passed on a few old clothes. His loyalty should be to his father.'

Chrissie snorted. 'Typical Paki values,' she said.

The words were like three cymbal clashes, reverberating round the shed long after the time it took to say them. Chrissie saw the ring of shocked faces looking at her and suddenly her rigid mask dissolved.

'Oh,' she said. 'Oh, I didn't want to say that. This break-in thing, it's left me in a state. Oh, Meena – '

'Why is it always Paki?' flared Meena. 'My family were from Gujerat, in India! Not Pakistan! And now, we are British! I was born here, but it's always, always Paki! "Go home Paki. We don't want you here, Paki".'

'Meena, I don't know why I said that. I couldn't help it – '

'Like you couldn't help having sex with a boy you didn't even like? What a pathetic reason for bringing a child into the world, because you couldn't say no!'

'I'm sorry,' choked Chrissie.

'It's Mouse you should say sorry to. He's better than all of us. He's done nothing wrong. All he's trying to do is protect his father.'

Chrissie began to cry. Rosa watched and felt nothing at all. A great tiredness crept over her and all she wanted was to be home, in her warm bed, asleep. 'Right,' she sighed. 'Now we've all said what was on our minds the only thing left to do is – what's the word – dissolve the Secrets Club. There's no point in us hanging around here any longer.'

For a few seconds no-one moved. Then Liam turned for the door.

'Mouse!' called Jason.

'Liam. Me name's Liam.'

'Liam. Please stay. Rosa, I'm sorry for what I said. Look everyone, don't go. We've got to plan our next move.'

'What next move? We can't do any more – except argue. Anyway, why are you so worried? That diary – it's going to send your reputation sky high.'

'No, it won't.'

'Pardon?'

'I was – lying. If I tell you, will you stay? Will you help me?' Jason looked round at each of them and, one by one, they looked to Rosa, waiting for her to decide. She hesitated. After what he had said to her, she wanted to walk out and leave him to suffer on his own.

'P-please . . .'

It was the stutter which swayed her. 'Go on, then. Tell us,' she said, switching on the moon lamp and collapsing on to a bean-bag.

Jason looked down at his hands, then up at the ceiling, blowing his hair from his eyes. 'Bit of a cliché, really,' he said. 'The lonely rich boy.' He attempted a charming grin but it wobbled into nothing. 'Because I am. I mean I was. Lonely. What can I say? Parties full of people and none of them listening. Boarding schools full of boys all trying to stay tough enough to get through the term.

'My dad, he's all right. If he walks into a room

137

and I'm there, he'll be pleased to see me. If he bumps into me on his way out, he might take me with him and we'll have a great time. But then he forgets me. When I'm not there, he doesn't miss me. For years I used to think, this time he'll remember my birthday, this time he'll come to the school open day . . . There's no malice in him. He just shouldn't've had a kid, because he's still a kid himself; a big kid who likes to play football.

'And then, there's my m-mother. How can I explain my mother?' Jason steepled his fingers together and frowned into the arch they made.

'Have you seen that glossy magazine, *House Beautiful*? My m-mother lives like she's in that magazine. Nothing out of place. New colour schemes every year. Everything matching. When I was little, I was just something that didn't match. I was a mess waiting to happen. She used to follow me round with a J-cloth. Do you see how she is?' Jason glanced up at Liam, who nodded politely.

'No. I can see I haven't explained her properly yet . . . OK. You know how little kids do paintings and their mums put them up on the wall? My mother would throw them in the bin. Then we went visiting and she saw how this woman had made a feature of her kids' drawings, putting them in frames and mixing them in with proper prints and things. The next day she went out and bought a load of frames and tried to get me to paint some pictures, only she kept saying, why don't you make that man's head smaller . . . why don't you make that look more like a tree . . . I threw the paints on her cream carpet. She sent me to boarding school.

That's why I only paint in here now. It's m-mine, my painting, and she can't have it.

'My gran was always there, though. My gran was special. She loved me. I used to buy her those tacky plaster ornaments little kids always go for and she would put them all up on the mantelpiece. My mother hated them. I thought I would go mad when Gran died. I used to tell her everything. That's when I started the diary – I had to unload it all somewhere.'

Jason ran his hands through his hair and jumped to his feet. 'And now D-cup's got it. All the poor me, and the bad poetry, and the pathetic whinges about my parents. If he lets that get around, I've had it. It'll be another bloody boarding school for me. No more privacy. No more painting. It took me ages to persuade her to let me come to Seaton Court. She only did it in the end because she thinks she's being fashionably liberal. If there's any hint of me not being a huge success, she'll send me away again. Do you see? It's too close to home for her: she has her image to think of.'

Rosa bowed her head, suddenly understanding all the boasting and the charm. His mother had him on trial. 'But, why didn't you tell us this before?' she asked.

'I was – embarrassed. It seemed to be such a stupid little secret. I suppose I was trying to look a bit more like a hero. I wanted to be strong, like you.'

'Me?' said Rosa, startled.

'I'd miss you,' he added, looking at Rosa. 'I'd miss you all, if I had to leave. Come on. So we all said stuff we didn't mean tonight. Not so surprising after what we'd just been through. Let's forget all that. Let's stick together for a bit longer. The worst has already happened. At least we can keep each other company. We might even come up with something else – we've got four days.'

'OK,' said Rosa and Jason gave her one of his shining smiles.

'So,' said Meena. 'Plan B. Any ideas?'

'Blow up the bungalow?' said Rosa.

Chrissie giggled. 'Arsenic on his chips?'

'Lock him in the Old House with the ghost?'

'Nah, the ghost'd leave home.'

'I've been down in that cellar,' said Liam, quietly, and the laughter stopped. 'He's got it all set up like a den. If he's still got the blackmail box, that's where it'll be.'

'Oh, Mouse, that's brilliant!' said Chrissie, a little too quickly.

'Me name's Liam.'

'Sorry, Liam.'

'The thing is,' said Rosa, 'That yard door's got a Yale lock on it – '

'There's another way in,' said Liam. 'I found it a few months ago. I'm in school more than you think. There's lots of warm places you can settle down in for the day, with no-one to bother you. You know that cleaners' store room on the ground floor? There's a sort of cupboard at the back of the room but it hasn't got a floor. It goes right down to another cupboard in the cellar.'

'A dumb waiter!' shrieked Chrissie.

'A what?' asked Meena.

'It's a sort of mini-lift. The cellar must've been the kitchen or the wine cellar or something, when it was still a house. They could send the food or the wine straight up to the butler.'

'There's none of that lift stuff left in it, just a little wooden shaft. I made a rope from dust sheets and climbed down. I could do that again and open the yard door from the inside for the rest of you to come in.'

They all looked at one another, hardly daring to hope that they had been given a second chance.

'When?' asked Jason.

'Tomorrow night!' crowed Rosa. 'There's a disco on in the main hall. Perfect cover – lots of noise!'

'All right,' said Meena. 'Let's get planning, I've got to be home in an hour.'

'But first, we'll celebrate,' said Jason, pulling a cardboard box from behind a bean-bag. 'We'll have a Secrets Club firework display! Everyone spread out round the edge of the room. Good. Now turn and face the walls. Right, here you are. Two each.'

Rosa looked down at the spray paint cans in her hands. 'Oh, no! Not over your mountain!'

'I was ready for a change, anyway. And a mountain's the perfect place for a firework display. Ready? Shake!'

The rattle of ball bearings filled the shed.

'And . . . Wait for it . . . Spray!'

Rosa sent a wavery orange streak running up the mountain. Chrissie squirted a lime green dot, then stopped. Meena did nothing; she was still trying to figure out which way to point the can. Liam wrote his name and then looked guilty.

'No, not like that,' cried Jason. 'Like this!' He sprayed an expansive sweep of crimson on to the

141

wall. 'And this!' He leapt high into the air to add a swirl of yellow.

The others laughed and began to copy him. Paint flared across the walls, bright and fresh, and they moved with the colours in a swooping, swaying dance, filling in all the spaces between them.

Date: Thursday, 6th November.
Time: Morning. Early. Six-ish.
Place: The mattress, my shed.

Dire Dearie,

I've got some bad news. Our cover's blown. I had to tell them – about us. It was either that or have the whole school reading the secret life of Jason Hughes on Monday morning. At least this way, I've still got a chance of staying at Seaton – as long as we find that box. What you call the lesser of two evils, only it wasn't as evil as I expected.

In fact, they were really good. There I was, s-s-s-s-s-s-stuttering away, waiting for them to throw up or have hysterics, but they sat and listened. Nobody walked out. Nobody told me I was a prat. And here's the most amazing part. Rosa Morgan changed, click, just like that! One minute she was looking at me like I was a piece of chewing gum stuck to her shoe, the next minute her beautiful eyes went all big and soft and she realized I was human after all. I wanted to kiss her.

I thought I'd blown it with Rosa when I called her a snob. I didn't mean it. I'd just had enough of the chewing gum treatment. She's not a snob. . . . well. . . . not really. She's more – stand-offish. I think it's because she's so busy being high-powered, she's forgotten how to be comfortable with people. Clever, hey? I wish I'd been so clever about the secret telling. I lied all this time because I thought she'd think I was an utter prat if she knew the truth – but holding back was the worst thing I could've done.

Please let us find this box tonight! I want to beat D-cup. I want to stay here. I want to get to know her.

Hello Josh. I beat you to it this morning. Look at me — all up and dressed. We'll still wrap up in our quilt, though, shall we, my Joshua? All wrapped up with your mum to have your bottle. There.

I've been watching you, while you were asleep. Yes, I have, smiler! I've been doing a lot of thinking, too. I was awful last night, Josh, the way I went for Mouse. And those things I said to Meena, that was my dad talking. I don't want to be like him. There'd been some trouble, you see, and you know how I hate any trouble. I think I was looking for someone to blame. Wimp of the year, as usual.

The thing is, Josh, you can't spend your life not wanting any trouble. Life doesn't work like that. Sometimes you've even got to start the trouble, if you want to change things. So, today I'm seeing that nice teacher, Mrs Sanderson, and I'm going to find out about using the creche if I stay on for A-levels. And I'm going to ask her who I should see about a place to live, in case things don't work out with your gran and grandpa. And you know what else? I'm going to send off my stories to some magazines. If I could get paid for them, I could start saving for us, Josh. For you and me.

Josh? Would you like to go into town with your mum on Saturday? We'll go on the bus, shall we? We could meet Rosa and everyone for a pizza and if we see anyone from school and they say is he your brother, I'm going to say, no, he's my baby. I am. Because Mum and Dad are wrong, Josh. I should be proud of you. And I want you to be proud of me. No secrets.

I'm still going tonight, though, and I'll be tough this time. The Secrets Club'll be glad of me tonight. You'll see.

Hello, Mum. It's me, Liam. It's nice up here, this time of the morning. The sun's out on the tops but it's still dark in the valley — I can see all the street lights on down there.

Mum. . . . the police have been round the house. Don't worry, nobody saw them. It was four o'clock this morning and Dad was at the door before they got to the real hammering. They took him up to the allotments. Mum, I was so scared. Dad said he'd be back soon, but I knew he wouldn't. It'd be straight to the nick when they found the stuff. I waited 'til the car was out of sight, then I ran. When I got there, the shed was empty, not a CD player in sight, and these two police were knee-deep in plant pots, looking fed up. Dad was standing there, cool as you like, offering them a cabbage each! He spied me through the hedge and gave me this great big wink.

I know just how you used to feel now, Mum, those times when you didn't know whether to kiss him or kill him. I was shaking and sweating and itching to land one on him, but there was this stupid grin on my face that wouldn't go away. . . . So I came straight up here to cool off. I don't understand any of it, except — it wasn't Andrew Greenwood who tipped off the police. They wouldn't've been looking in plant pots if it was Andrew: they'd've known it was CD players.

I'm still going tonight, to the school. I'll not have them saying I let them down. They're a funny lot, Mum. The things they worry about — like why their mums didn't put their paintings on the wall when they were kids. And when they give you something, they don't forget it; it's not just pass it on like we do on the estate. Anyway, Dad's all right. I knew you'd want to know. Goodbye, Mum.

God Bless.

OK Meena. A few circuits to warm up, then a sprint. Knock a couple of seconds off and you're in with a chance to run at County level. It's a great morning for running. Cold, but not too cold. Good, clear sky and the air as pure as you'll get it all day. Find your stride. Settle in. . .

. . . There's nothing like getting caught in someone else's house to clear the mind. I've been so silly, doing a whole lot of new bad things just to keep one bad thing quiet. What if she'd called the police? It was D-cup — he made the cheating seem so awful. He made it seem like a dreadful crime I had to hide. . . .

. . . Not at the track, Meena. He's not allowed at the track, remember. Watch the breathing. . . .

. . . I really let them down in the bungalow with that . . . that noise. Jason said she was on to us anyway, but I think he was only being kind. Afterwards, when Mouse gave us the message, I was almost relieved. At least it'll all be over soon. It won't be so bad, people knowing. Really. The Secrets Club — they didn't think it was so terrible. . . .

Look at Dad, over on that bench, shivering with cold and half-asleep. How many times has he taken me out for early morning training? He never complains. I've been so busy trying to protect my family. How ashamed they would be if they knew I broke into another person's house, trying to protect them. All they want is for me to be happy here. They expect a lot, yes, but they love me. I'm so lucky. Look at Jason, look at Chrissie. Who is there to wish them happiness?

And Mouse. I'll go tonight, for Mouse. Then I get back to being me. Right, come on, Meena. Get that time down! Go!

>Insert a disc
>Opening document file
>File name: Rosa

Jason likes me!!!! I just wanted to see it, up on the screen. Jason likes me. Six o'clock. Three hours before I see him at school. I couldn't sleep after last night. What a night it was! Break-ins and bust-ups and Jason saying he would miss me if he had to go away.

I nearly told him about the photo right then but, I don't know, it doesn't seem important now. He's not like I thought he was at all. It took me a long time to see it. Maybe he was right, about the labels. I'm not a snob, though. Am I?

D-cup can do what he likes with that photo. I don't care any more. I never thought I'd say that! I'm still going tonight, though. It was me who started the Secrets Club, so I'm going to be there at the finish. I hope we find the box, for everyone else's sake. And I want to get that vicious bully. That's one label I didn't get wrong. D-cup is a bully.

I'm dreading it, going into that cellar. D-cup's den. We've all stood outside that door, wondering what was down those steps. It'll be worth it, though, if we find Jason's diary. Then he can stay at Seaton and maybe . . . well. . . .

But first, I've got to go and do my paper round, and ordinary things like that.

Jason likes me!

>Delete file name: Rosa
>Are you sure? Yes/No
>Yes

10
The Cage

Liam was back in his old clothes. Rosa could see the white rings round his trouser bottoms as he leaned into the cupboard and peered down the lift shaft. She felt a twist of guilt, sharp as a lemon slice, and grimaced.

'Turn the light off a minute,' said Liam.

Rosa flicked the wall switch and stood in the darkness of the store room, listening to the steam-hammer thump of the disco in the main hall.

'OK. Back on.' Liam climbed down from the cupboard, grinning. 'The cellar's empty all right. No light coming through at all. I'll get started. You keep watch.'

Rosa nodded and slipped out of the store room into the corridor that linked the Old House to the main hall. The swing doors at the end of the corridor flew open and music blasted out, making her jump. She looked up and froze. A trestle table had been set up just inside the hall and two women stood behind it, selling drinks. One of them was Mrs Greenwood. Rosa stared, transfixed, but Mrs Greenwood did not look up from her work. Seconds later the doors banged shut behind a group of laughing girls and Rosa slumped against the wall.

The girls headed for the toilets next to the store room and she smiled and nodded at them, trying to look casual.

As soon as the corridor was empty, Rosa eased back into the store room. Liam was gone. She stared down the shaft and shivered, imaging him moving through the dark cellar with his torch bringing shadows to life. Quickly, she pulled the dust-sheet rope from the lift shaft and bundled it into a corner. Then she shut the cupboard doors, checked the room and turned off the light. A minute later, she was back in the corridor, waiting for her heart to stop pounding.

The next time the swing doors opened, it was Jason. Nine o'clock, dead on time, thought Rosa, glancing at her watch. Jason turned to yell something back into the hall, then bounced along the corridor towards her, laughing. She squashed her irritation. That was precisely why they had chosen him to check out the hall, because he would be able to look as though he was enjoying himself.

Close to, she could see the strain in his face. The skin was too pale, the eyes too bright. Sweat trickled at his hairline. 'No sign of D-cup. You go on. I'll only be a minute,' he said, disappearing into the boys' toilets.

Rosa took a deep breath and padded from the corridor into the entrance hall of the Old House. Evening classes had been moved to C-block, because of the disco, and the house was empty and dark. Rosa took a few steps across the wooden floor and stopped. The stair lion on the bannister-end was looking at her.

Rosa gasped and clenched her fists. The lion

149

gleamed softly in the light that spilled through from the corridor. Two points of light danced in its wooden eyes. She took another step. The points of light moved.

Look, it's a wooden lion, stupid, thought Rosa. Just walk across the hall and out through the yard door. Simple.

She tried to take another step but her feet refused to move. A disco was in full swing a corridor away, but Rosa was alone, trapped in a four-year-old nightmare. Wood creaked. The last of her courage seeped away and she closed her eyes.

'Rosa,' hissed Chrissie from the yard door. Wood creaked again as she took another step into the hall. 'Come on. Liam's got the door open and me and Meena are freezing, waiting in that yard.'

Chrissie hurried out again and Rosa glared at the lion. She marched to the bottom of the stairs and poked it in the eye. 'So much for you!' she hissed and ran out into the yard after Chrissie.

The concrete steps beyond the green door were in darkness. Automatically Rosa reached round the corner for the light switch and a hand closed over her wrist. Her mouth opened in soundless shock. It had caught her at last, the Thing that breathed in the dark trees outside her window and lurked under her bed, waiting for a dangling foot. All the years of missing out the creaky stair-tread on her way to bed, or closing her cupboard door before the light went out counted for nothing now. She had touched a stair lion and the Thing had come to claim her.

'Leave the light, Rosa,' whispered Meena, appearing in the doorway.

'Oh! Oh, it's you!'

'Sorry, did I give you a shock?'

Rosa shrugged her shoulders and took a shaky breath, pushing childhood monsters from her mind. They were dealing with a real monster now; a monster with a weight problem and an earring; a monster who did ordinary things like eating fish and chips and going home to mum every night.

'We're leaving the light off,' explained Meena. 'We've got two torches here to use when Jason arrives. Where is he?'

'Here,' whispered Jason behind Rosa and she just managed not to jump.

They made their way down the concrete steps and stood in a cluster at the bottom. The two torch beams flicked around the cellar, giving Rosa fragmented images of flagstones, brick walls, and a web of steel girders and pipes above their heads.

'What if we all move round together?' suggested Chrissie. 'Two to hold the torches steady and three to search?'

'Good idea,' whispered Meena.

They followed the wall past a tangled pile of broken chairs and a hulking metal cylinder. 'The old boiler,' whispered Liam, holding his torch high for Rosa to check behind it. 'Everything's heated from the new boiler house now; this place is hardly used any more.'

The insistent thud of the disco grew louder as they reached the cupboard doors hiding the dumb waiter, then faded as they shuffled on. Next came a whole section of wall protected by a wire mesh cage which reached from floor to ceiling. Behind the mesh were ranks of water pipes and stopcocks and neatly labelled fuse boxes with thick cables sprouting from them. The door of the cage was padlocked but they didn't need to open it. They could see there was no box.

'It's got to be here somewhere,' groaned Jason. 'Only one more wall, then we're back at the stairs!'

'His den,' said Liam, letting his torch beam settle on the corner where the wall met the stairs. 'It used to be the caretaker's base, I think, when the Old House was a girls' school.' Meena's torch beam joined Liam's and they all saw the big old desk stacked with beer cans. An arm chair sagged beside the desk and a mirror had been propped above the wall phone, surrounded by smiling page three girls.

'All the comforts of life,' said Jason, then stopped, pointing to the space between the chair and the desk. 'What's that?'

In the concentrated torch light, the box corner shone dully. 'We've found it,' breathed Chrissie.

Footsteps echoed on the flagstones of the yard above them; slow, heavy feet in boots with metal toe caps, coming towards the green door.

'Oh, no,' whimpered Rosa.

They scattered, torch beams tracing wild patterns. By the time the key slotted into the door, the cellar was dark, quiet and apparently empty. The lights came on, mercilessly bright, and Rosa realized what a stupid hiding place she had chosen, right in the middle of his den. She squeezed herself further behind the arm chair as Andrew clattered down the stairs and headed straight for her.

Fssstt! A ring pull hit the floor beneath the desk and Rosa listened as he chugged down half a can of beer in one go. Matches rattled in their box. A scrape. A flaring hiss. Cigarette smoke curled under her nose. She braced herself, waiting for the chair back to crush her against the wall as he sat down. Instead an arm appeared in the top corner of her vision and adjusted the mirror above the wall 'phone.

'OK, you down there,' said Andrew. Rosa felt the hairs rise on the nape of her neck. She waited for him to reach down and drag her out.

'Uh, I'd like to play a new song for all of you, down there in the auditorium,' said Andrew, in a dreadful American accent. 'Ready, girls?'

He's talking to his page three photos, thought Rosa and relief stormed through her.

'Dangawangawangdangdangdang,' twanged Andrew, sounding remarkably like an electric guitar. Then he began to scream in an excited falsetto 'Oh, Andrew, give me your autograph! Oh, Andie, give me a lock of your hair! Oooh, Randy Andie, give me your underpants!'

Rosa covered her mouth and nose with her hand, pressing hard.

'Sorry, girls. Time to check out the talent upstairs,' said Andrew, blowing a kiss at the mirror. He headed for the steps and Meena tensed in her hiding place behind the boiler. The torch in her hand twitched, tapping the curving metal, and the boiler gave off a hollow clang. Meena jumped and a second, louder clang rang out. In the dreadful silence which followed, Rosa completely lost the urge to laugh.

Andrew's face darkened as he realized that his performance had been seen. 'Come out of there,' he grated, in a voice like splintering glass.

Meena huddled, silently.

'If I have to come and get you. . . .' warned Andrew.

Meena sensed Chrissie stiffen beside her. With a sigh, she eased crab-like from behind the boiler and walked over to Andrew.

'Aha. The cheat,' he said, spinning her round and wrenching her arm up between her shoulder blades. Meena yelped.

'Come on. Who else?' shouted Andrew, yanking her wrist.

'No-one,' gasped Meena.

'Come out, come out wherever you are!' called Andrew. He pulled on Meena's arm hard enough to force a scream.

'Leave her alone!' shouted Liam, opening the doors of the cupboard and clambering from the shaft. The purple and yellow bruising around his eye stood out against his pale skin.

'Oh, good evening, Liam,' said Andrew, in a conversational tone which hung balanced for a moment over his cold, gleaming fury, like a tea cosy on the tip of a sword. Then Andrew gave up on the pleasantries. 'Does your thieving dad know he's got a Paki-lover for a son?' he screamed, dragging Meena over to the steel mesh cage. He unhooked the key ring from his belt and opened the padlock. 'In,' he ordered Liam, swinging the door wide.

Chrissie saw her chance. She edged out on the far side of the boiler and, while Andrew was clicking the padlock shut on Meena and Liam, she made a break for it.

Andrew whirled around.

Rosa jumped up from behind the chair.

'Go on, Chrissie!' she screamed.

The distraction worked. Andrew faltered just long enough for Chrissie to make the stairs before he could cut her off.

'Yes!' shouted Rosa, as Chrissie pounded up the steps. There was no way Andrew could reach the stairs, swing round the corner and climb the steps in time to stop her.

'Yes!' shouted Rosa again, waving her arms. Then she stopped in mid-wave as Andrew launched himself at the side of the staircase. One hand hooked over the metal railing, the other clamped on to Chrissie's ankle. Then he let himself drop back to the cellar floor. Chrissie screamed as his weight dragged her after him. The edge of the concrete staircase scraped the length of her spine as she slipped under the rail. She fell heavily on the flagstones at Andrew's feet and lay gasping, her face screwed up against the flaring pain in her back.

'You – ' Rosa was running before she knew it, carried on a surge of anger. She leapt on to Andrew's back and grabbed a fistful of his frizzy hair, screaming all the while. Andrew simply slammed an elbow into her belly. Rosa's diaphragm went into spasm, cutting off her screams. Silently, she slid off his back and folded up on the floor, concentrating on the problem of getting some air into her lungs. Andrew was putting Chrissie into the cage, but that was all right. Anything was all right as long as Rosa could be left alone to find a way to breathe again.

At last, her diaphragm let a tiny gulp of air get through. She sucked greedily, forcing more air down and, grudgingly, her lungs began to work.

'In you go, bird-mess,' said Andrew, somewhere

155

above her. Then she was behind the mesh, clutching her ribs and making strangled whooping noises with every breath. Chrissie rubbed at her back.

'I'm all right,' said Rosa, forcing herself to stand straight.

Andrew was prowling the cellar. He searched the pile of broken chairs, the boiler, the lift shaft and his den. There was nowhere else to look.

'Where's the fifth one?' he demanded, standing in front of the cage.

'H-he got away,' said Chrissie. 'He's probably getting someone right now. You'd better let us out.'

Andrew shook his head. 'I would've heard if he'd tried to run. I would've seen.' He said it with such solid confidence that Rosa found herself wanting to nod in agreement, as though it was an indisputable fact.

'Where is he?' repeated Andrew.

Rosa's head was reeling. Jason had disappeared and she couldn't explain it. All she knew was that they had to come up with something that would satisfy Andrew. Jason was their only chance now. 'He. . . . wouldn't come,' she said, bowing her head. 'When I 'phoned, he said he'd had enough of kids' games.'

Andrew laughed. 'Ahh, poor little bird-mess. He was right, though. That's just what you're doing – playing kids' games. You're pathetic! Why didn't you put the door on the latch so I couldn't come in and find you? Why didn't you all jump me when you had the chance?'

They stood in a line in the narrow mesh cage, not knowing what to say. Rosa raised her eyes to the ceiling and looked straight at Jason. He was lying on his belly along the top of one of the steel girders that criss-crossed the roof space. All this time he had been hiding in plain view, if anyone had thought to look up. As she stared, he eased himself along the girder, inching nearer to Andrew. Thick, grey feathers of dust floated down to land on the flagstones. A flap of lagging shook free from a water pipe and dangled from a thread.

Rosa jerked her head down and stared hard at Andrew, eyes wide. Behind her, water pipes sighed and the fuse boxes hummed steadily. Above her a girder creaked.

'Don't talk to me about kids' games, Mr Guitar Man!' she blurted. 'Oh, Andie, give me a lock of your hair!' she mocked as Jason went into a crouch above Andrew's head. 'Ooh, Andrew give me your autograph!'

Andrew threw himself against the cage in a fury, kicking and slamming at the mesh centimetres from her face. When he fell back, panting, Jason dropped from the girder like a stone.

Seconds later, Andrew was face down on the flagstones and Jason was sitting on his back with one knee digging into his neck. Andrew's arm was twisted up between his shoulder blades and Jason was bending the fingers back as well, just to be sure.

Slowly, Jason reached down to Andrew's belt and unhooked the keys. His face was grim. Rosa could see it took all his strength to keep Andrew down. She held her breath.

Jason leaned towards her, holding out the keys and she pushed her arm through the mesh as far as it would go. Andrew heaved and Jason had to pull back, wrenching at his fingers until he grunted and lay still.

'I'll have to throw them,' said Jason. He brought back his arm and flung the keys at the cage but they bounced against the mesh and landed on the flagstones outside. Liam was the nearest. The others shuffled together, giving him as much room as they could in the confined space. Liam kneeled down, pushed back the sleeve of his ski jacket and slid his arm through as far as the elbow. The keys were just out of reach.

Andrew swivelled his head to watch. 'Come on!' gritted Jason, fighting to keep his knee on the thick, bull neck.

Liam forced his arm a little further through the mesh until his middle finger was touching a key. Slowly, he began to scrape the key ring nearer.

'Want to know a secret? Rosa Morgan's got the hots for Jason Hughes!' yelled Andrew. Jason's head came up and his shocked eyes met hers. His grip slackened and Andrew surged from the floor, flinging him off. Liam screamed as Andrew jumped on his hand. The keys span away, out of reach.

Jason scrambled up and ran after them but suddenly Andrew's foot was in his way, kicking at his ankles. Then the stone floor smacked him in the head.

'See?' crowed Andrew, holding up the polaroid snap. Jason glowered from the cage.

'I'm so sorry,' said Rosa. 'I meant to tell you all, but first it was too important and then, well, it didn't seem important at all. . . .'

'It's all right, Rosa,' said Jason, still glaring at Andrew. 'No blame. No blame, understand?'

'Ahh. Sweet. You'll be the first, bird-mess. This photo, on the main notice board, Monday morning.'

'Go ahead! I don't care any more about your stupid photo!'

Andrew frowned. Then his face cleared and he smiled.

'All right,' he said, moving to the wall 'phone. 'I'll just have a chat with the officers at the local nick, shall I Liam?'

They all turned to Liam, horror written on their faces. Liam was smiling.

'Too late,' he said. 'Some other grass got there first. They've already been to the allotments. My dad gave them a nice cabbage each. It's true,' he added, turning to the others. 'They didn't find a thing. My dad's in the clear.'

'Oh, Liam!' Meena hugged him and he looked over her shoulder at Andrew, with a broad grin on his face.

'Brilliant!' crowed Jason.

Andrew looked at Meena and opened his mouth.

'And don't even try the cheat thing with me,' she said, her eyes sparking. 'I've had enough. You'll have to buy your beer from now on. Only don't try to buy it from our off-licences, because my father and my uncle and my brothers are going to be out for your blood when I tell them what you've been doing.'

Suddenly elation caught them. They were trapped in a tiny cage, with high-power cables humming at their backs and D-cup pacing the floor in front of them. It should have been a nightmare, but they were laughing and hugging, united and strong. Andrew had lost them.

'Oh, dear,' said Rosa. 'You are having a bad night.'

'Shut up!' roared Andrew. 'Unless you want the whole school to know about that tart and her baby!'

Chrissie shook back her hair and gave Andrew a cool look. 'I'm taking Josh into town on Saturday,' she said, turning to the others. 'It's about time I started showing him off. Want to join me for lunch?'

'I wouldn't miss it,' said Jason.

'Count me in,' said Meena.

'And me.'

'Yeah, me too.'

They turned to face Andrew. He was standing beside the box. Jason's diary hung from his finger-tips. His face was flushed. 'Let's talk about this, then, shall we?' he hissed, glaring at them.

Rosa sensed Jason tense beside her. They were silent.

Andrew waited. 'No fancy speeches, Hughesie? No clever remarks? I tell you what I'll do. It's a shame to make you wait 'till Monday, so I'm going to nip up to the office right now, photocopy some of the best bits, and set up a notice board right outside the main hall. Then everyone can have a good read when they leave the disco. After that, you'll be free to go. Make yourselves comfortable. I'll be back.'

D-cup grinned and turned for the stairs. Jason gripped the mesh. 'A-Andrew,' he said.

'Yes?' said Andrew, stopping with one foot on the bottom step. Jason was silent.

'Oh, go on,' chided Andrew. 'Don't be shy. I like a good plead. No?' He began to walk up the stairs.

'D-cup!' yelled Rosa.

'Don't call me that,' began Andrew, spinning to face her. 'I don't – ' He stopped in mid-sentence as he realized what she was about to do.

'One more step,' said Rosa, her fingers gripping the switch for the main fuse box. 'One more step and I'll pull this switch. That'll stop the disco don't you think? That'll bring them all down here to fix the fuse. The Head. The teachers. Your dad – '

A spasm crossed Andrew's face.

'Yes,' continued Rosa. 'Your dad'll probably be the first one down. It's the caretaker's job, fixing fuses.'

Andrew hesitated, then turned and came back down into the cellar. 'Stalemate,' he said. 'For now. But I can wait until the end of the disco.' He moved to his chair and sat down, opening a can of beer. Rosa swallowed, suddenly dreadfully thirsty.

'Let's have some entertainment, shall we? While we wait?' He picked up the diary and began to read in a quavering little voice. One by one, Jason's most secret thoughts were lifted from the page and laid out, pale and trembling on the cold cellar floor. The poem he wrote about death, after his gran's funeral; his worries about spots and the shape of his nose; his joy when his dad remembered him, and his pain when his dad forgot. Andrew read them all out, relentlessly. Jason rested his head against the mesh of the cage, shoulders slumped. The others stood, wordless, their elation gone.

Then Chrissie raised her head and began to sing in a surprisingly rich, clear voice. She chose the first song that came into her head and her voice soared through the opening lines, growing stronger with every note. Andrew faltered in his reading, then continued in a louder voice. Chrissie kept singing.

The others lifted their heads and stared at her. Come on, come on, she thought. Join in please! She waved her hands at them like a conductor but still they just stared. Oh, God, they're not going to. It's because I chose a corny song. They're too embarrassed. What do they want at a time like this, opera? It is a corny song, though. It's a dreadful song. Why can I never do anything right?

Chrissie's voice trembled and began to lose power. Then, raggedly at first, they began to join in, until they were all singing at the tops of their voices.

'Walk on, walk on, with hope in your heart, and you'll never walk alone!'

Andrew dropped the diary and jumped from his seat, shouting at them to stop, but they carried on, making the schmaltzy words bounce off the ceiling. 'You'll never walk alone!'

Andrew raged at them through the bars but his voice was drowned out. He ran to the pile of broken chairs and grabbed a stave of wood, then he crashed it again and again against the cage, in a crazed accompaniment. Splinters flew, but they kept singing until Jason looked up and stopped. One by one the others saw what he had seen. The singing came to a halt. They gazed at the stairs.

Mrs Greenwood was standing half way down, clutching the metal handrail. Her face, as she stared at her son, was full of shame and sorrow.

'Andrew,' she said.

D-cup stopped. His arm, raised for another blow, trembled. 'Mum!' he said, recovering. 'I was just going to 'phone Dad. I found this lot down here trying to steal – ' He faltered for a moment, gazing around the cellar. 'Um, trying to get to the fuses. Planning to ruin the disco!' A self-righteous note crept into his voice. 'Planning to turn out the lights!'

'So you locked them in – with the fuses,' said Mrs Greenwood, flatly.

'I'll – just get Dad.' Andrew moved to the 'phone and started to dial. Dark wings of sweat stained the back of his T-shirt.

'All right, Andrew,' said Mrs Greenwood, coming down into the cellar. 'And when you've finished, I'll talk to him. I'll talk to him about how the old Gym burned down five years ago.'

Andrew dropped the receiver as though it was electrified. He stared at his mother and the blood drained from his face.

'I'll talk to him about the way you burst into the house that night, twenty minutes before we saw the flames. I'll tell him about the singe marks and the stink of burning on your clothes when I came to wash them. I'll tell him about you crying in your sleep for weeks afterwards.'

'They said it was a cigarette left in the waste-paper bin,' said Andrew, wiping the sweat from his upper lip. 'They said it wasn't arson because all the windows and doors were locked and all the glass was blown out with the heat, not smashed in. . . .'

'You used your dad's keys, Andrew. For the first time. But not the last. Those are copies you've had

163

cut, I suppose,' she said, pointing to the ring of keys at his belt. Andrew cupped his hand over the key-ring and Mrs Greenwood watched him, waiting for the next lie.

'I – I didn't mean to do it,' quavered Andrew. 'Not burn it down. I just wanted to get back at Mr Grindley for calling me . . . for calling me. . . .'

'D-cup,' sighed Mrs Greenwood.

'I only wanted to burn his tracksuit, but it got out of control and it wouldn't – I couldn't – He shouldn't've called me that,' finished Andrew, regaining some of his fight.

'So much like your dad,' said Mrs Greenwood and her voice was sad, not proud. Andrew seemed to shrink then, as she stared at him. He dropped his head, sullen in defeat. She watched him for a moment longer, with a look of resignation on her face, as though she was finally letting herself see what her son was like. 'I should've done something then,' she said to herself. 'I was just hoping. . . .'

Rosa stared out through the mesh, unable to rid herself of the feeling that it was Andrew and his mother trapped in the cage, with her looking in.

'I saw you leave the disco,' said Mrs Greenwood, turning to face Rosa and Jason. 'Then I saw him, going the same way. So I followed. I heard most of it.'

They watched her, mesmerized. Rosa was gripping the front of the cage so hard, her fingers turned blue.

'You owe me one – for last night,' said Mrs Greenwood. 'I could've called the police.'

Rosa nodded, understanding.

'We won't say anything,' said Jason.

Mrs Greenwood stared at them for a long moment, deciding. 'I'm going to trust you,' she said. 'And you can trust me to make sure he won't do this to anyone again, all right?'

Rosa nodded again, hardly daring to breathe.

'Let them out,' said Mrs Greenwood to Andrew.

'But – '

'Let them out!'

Andrew unlocked the door, refusing to look at them as they filed out.

'Give them their – things.'

Andrew kicked the box over to them and they took back their secrets.

'Now, give me the keys.'

Andrew closed his fist around the keys and shook his head. Mrs Greenwood held out her hand.

'No, Mum. I can't do without these – '

'Leave us alone, will you?' said Mrs Greenwood to the others, without taking her eyes off Andrew.

Rosa turned to thank Mrs Greenwood as they filed past, then thought better of it. They climbed from the cellar, leaving mother and son facing one another across the silent room. Meena pulled the green door shut and they stood in a circle in the Old House yard, their breath pluming in the fresh, cold air. Stars sparkled above. The disco still thudded on in the main hall. The whole thing had taken less than an hour.

Nobody spoke about what had happened in the cellar. It was too big a thing to talk about straight away. Liam hugged the CD player to his chest and thought about stopping at the chippie on the way home to his dad. Chrissie pictured Josh asleep in

165

his cot, and suddenly yearned to be stroking the perfect curve of his cheek.

'It's finished,' breathed Meena.

Rosa and Jason looked at one another and smiled.

. . . Andrew curled under the covers like a baby, trying to pretend it had never happened. He ducked his head beneath the duvet and jammed his pillow over the top, but still the noise leaked in from the top of the hill. Sirens bawled, men shouted, glass shattered and rafters snapped like giant matchsticks, but all that was nothing compared to the noises of the fire. It roared and bellowed on the dark hill like an angry bear.

With a sob, Andrew threw back the covers and crept towards the flickering brightness behind his curtains. He peered through the gap to the top of the hill. Flames were dancing at the gym windows and tongues of fire rose above the roof, licking oxygen from the sky. Great billows of smoke rolled with the wind, hiding the Old House completely. As he watched, the flat roof caved in and the gym seemed to grow taller as a solid column of fire erupted from within.

Andrew moaned. Tears rolled down his face, each filled with little, leaping flames. This was not what he wanted. Not at all. The fire held no attraction for him. He had only wanted to get back at Grindley for calling him. . . . He hadn't meant to. . . . But, even as he shook, filled with the terror of being caught, his hand strayed to his belt where, for a short while, the keys had been clipped. He missed the weight of them swinging from their long chain. He remembered the way they had bumped against his thigh, jangling softly in time with his footsteps as he walked through the dark gym. And such walking! For once, he had moved with a sure grace, carrying his bulk like a dancer. He had not been lonely with the keys at his side, even though he was alone. For a short time, he had stopped being an outsider.

Andrew thought about the keys and what he could do with them. He could look inside the lockers of the girls in his class. They might shut him out during the day, with their cool stares, but the keys would open up their secrets for him. He could step through the staffroom door and explore the teachers' bolt-holes as the wall clocks ticked the night away. Then the next time they humiliated him in their lessons, he would know how to hurt them back. After all, he was thirteen years old now and he knew he looked older – it was time they started giving him some respect! He could even walk into the Head's office without knocking. He could sit in Mr Carshaw's chair and rest his feet, in the trainers that Mr Carshaw had banned, on the desk blotter. . . .

Andrew watched the gym burn down and thought about the next time it would be safe to borrow his father's keys. The tears dried on his cheeks and his lips curved in a smile as he dreamed about how he would clip the keys to his belt and walk through the school, his school, with the confidence of belonging.

Other great reads from **Red Fox**

Further Red Fox titles that you might enjoy reading are listed on the following pages. They are available in bookshops or they can be ordered directly from us.

If you would like to order books, please send this form and the money due to:

ARROW BOOKS, BOOKSERVICE BY POST, PO BOX 29, DOUGLAS, ISLE OF MAN, BRITISH ISLES. Please enclose a cheque or postal order made out to Arrow Books Ltd for the amount due, plus 75p per book for postage and packing to a maximum of £7.50, both for orders within the UK. For customers outside the UK, please allow £1.00 per book.

NAME_____

ADDRESS_____

_____

Please print clearly.

Whilst every effort is made to keep prices low, it is sometimes necessary to increase cover prices at short notice. If you are ordering books by post, to save delay it is advisable to phone to confirm the correct price. The number to ring is THE SALES DEPARTMENT 071 (if outside London) 973 9700.

Other great reads ✦ *from* **Red Fox**

Superb historical stories from Rosemary Sutcliff

Rosemary Sutcliff tells the historical story better than anyone else. Her tales are of times filled with high adventure, desperate enterprises, bloody encounters and tender romance. Discover the vividly real world of Rosemary Sutcliff today!

THE CAPRICORN BRACELET
ISBN 0 09 977620 0   £2.50

KNIGHT'S FEE
ISBN 0 09 977630 8   £2.99

THE SHINING COMPANY
ISBN 0 09 985580 1   £3.50

THE WITCH'S BRAT
ISBN 0 09 975080 5   £2.50

SUN HORSE, MOON HORSE
ISBN 0 09 979550 7   £2.50

TRISTAN AND ISEULT
ISBN 0 09 979550 7   £2.99

BEOWULF: DRAGON SLAYER
ISBN 0 09 997270 0   £2.50

THE HOUND OF ULSTER
ISBN 0 09 997260 3   £2.99

THE LIGHT BEYOND THE FOREST
ISBN 0 09 997450 9   £2.99

THE SWORD AND THE CIRCLE
ISBN 0 09 997460 6   £2.99